CHARLES OMOLE

Author: Prosperity UnLeashed

BREAKTHROUGH STRATEGIES

FOR CHRISTIANS IN THE

Marketplace

Biblical Guide to the Strategic Invasion & Reclaim of the Marketplace

The Marketplace is a spiritual entity; and money flows in the direction of spiritual power, either Godly or Satanic. Only those that are strong in God will be able to dislodge the economic system of Babylon. The final Battle for souls have begun....

The marketplace is a spiritual entity. Money flows in the direction of spiritual power, either godly or satanic. Only those who are strong in God will be able to dislodge the economic system of Babylon. The final battle for souls has begun.

BREAKTHROUGH STRATEGIES FOR CHRISTIANS IN THE MARKETPLACE

A biblical guide to the strategic invasion and reclamation of the marketplace.

Charles Omole
Author of *Prosperity Unleashed*

Copyright © 2013
By Charles Omole

Published by:

WINNING FAITH
OUTREACH MINISTRIES

London . New York . Lagos

ISBN: 978-1-907095-09-2

All rights reserved under international copyright law. Contents must not be reproduced in whole or in part, or in any form for profit, without the written consent of the author.

Most Scriptures are from the New Kings James version of the Bible, with a few from the New International Version. All rights duly acknowledged.

DEDICATION:

The book is dedicated to *all* the champions of faith in the secular arena. Stay strong! The Lord will soon place all your enemies under your feet.

CONTENTS

Introduction -- 9

Chapter 1
Ruler of this world's darkness -- 25

Chapter 2
A new mind needed for battle -- 41

Chapter 3
Understanding and developing a new mind for the marketplace battle -- 59

Chapter 4
Our calling to the marketplace -- 131

Chapter 5
Overview of the spirituality of the marketplace

Chapter 6
How did we get here? How Christians lost the mountains -- *171*

Chapter 7
Breakthrough strategies in the **Media** -- 189

Chapter 8
Breakthrough strategies in the area of
Government. -- 211

Chapter 9
Breakthrough strategies in the **Education** sector -- 229

Chapter 10
Breakthrough strategies in the **Economy / business** sector -- 253

Chapter 11
Breakthrough strategies in **Arts, entertainment, movies, fashion & related** sectors -- 289

Chapter 12
Breakthrough strategies in the **Religion / Religious Arena** -- 311

Chapter 13
Breakthrough strategies in **Family** life -- 331

Chapter 14
Becoming a **Mountain Taker** -- 347

INTRODUCTION

The Scriptures make it abundantly clear that God has more to say and more secrets than the Bible contains. In fact, the apostle John said that not everything Jesus said and did was recorded.

"And there are also many other things that Jesus did, which if they were written one by one, I suppose that even the world itself could not contain the books that would be written. Amen." **–John 21:25 (NKJV)**

So God through the Holy Spirit inspired the biblical authors to write enough to get us rooted in God; but God is still in the business of speaking new things and revealing new mysteries to this generation in the right season.

Of course every new word must agree with the Scripture as written, if it is indeed from God. The Bible is God's sure word of prophecy, and all "new" revelation must agree with the *logos* word of God that we already have. But without doubt God still speaks new revelation as the Bible demonstrates.

The apostle Paul said in Ephesians, for example:

For this reason I, Paul, the prisoner of Christ Jesus for you Gentiles— ² if indeed you have heard of the dispensation of the grace of God which was given to me for you, ³ how that by revelation he made known to me the mystery.... which in other ages was not made known to the sons of men, as it has now been revealed by the Spirit to his holy apostles and prophets: ⁶ that the Gentiles should be fellow heirs of the same body, and partakers of his promise in Christ through the gospel, ⁷ of which I became a minister according to the gift of the grace of God given to me by the effective working of his power. **–Ephesians 3:1-7**

Up till that time the Jews were not expecting the Gentiles to be part of the kingdom. In fact all the apostles of the Lamb who were with Jesus centred their ministry on the Jews. After all, Christ himself said he was sent to the lost sheep of the house of *Israel*.

Even Jesus did not reveal the full picture to his disciples at the start of his ministry, because they could not have handled it at that time. So when the time was right, God revealed his eternal secret and released a *new* grace upon the apostle Paul to pioneer a ministry (to the

Gentiles) that had not existed before. In fact many of the other apostles, especially Peter, initially resisted Paul's ministry to the Gentiles. It was, after all, a departure from the norm they knew.

So we can be sure God reveals new secrets to his tested servants (apostles and prophets) in order to advance his purpose on earth. We are now at such a time in the kingdom of God. The Lord is now releasing the understanding of the operations of the marketplace to his tested servants as we move into a season of strategic invasion and reclamation of that place. The kingdoms of this world will become the kingdoms of our Lord and of his Christ as stated in Scripture.

On 1 January 2009 God gave me the vision for a fresh ministry mandate. The Lord said:
"It is the dawn of a new season for you and it is time to move to the next level. The time has come to empower my people to reach confidently beyond the walls of the church into the structures of Babylon, to redeem not only the persons in it but also its systems. For my glory is about to be revealed in the marketplaces of the earth. This will herald my promise of wealth transfer and the end of the age."

I did not fully understand this new mandate until few months later, when the devil began to throw at me everything he had, to take me out. At the same time God began to open my eyes to breath-taking revelations. He also gave me spiritual insight into the satanic operations of the marketplace. That year marked the beginning for me of a three-year spiritual battle with Satan that almost cost me my life. But God enabled me to be victorious. The he revealed to me, the more I began to understand why Satan wanted me out.

The enemy does not want this revelation to be disseminated and established in the kingdom, since it will dispossess him of his last bastion and control centre, the marketplace.

So you will be blessed as you read this. Get ready to be transformed by the power of God's word as the secrets of the operations of the marketplace are revealed and a revival is declared upon God's church.

Let us start from where it all began. In the beginning God made humankind. He spoke into existence both the human remit on the earth and the equipment with which to dominate it. But the tools and equipment were spiritual in nature, rather than physical. Why? Because the man God was speaking to had no physical form.

The man God commanded to be fruitful and multiply was still entirely spiritual. It was spirit-to-spirit communication. What does the Word of God say?

And God said, "Let us make man in our image, after our likeness: and let them have dominion over the fish of the sea, and over the fowl of the air, and over the cattle, and over all the earth, and over every creeping thing that creepeth upon the earth." 27 So God created man in his own image, in the image of God created he him; male and female created he them. 28 And God blessed them, and God said unto them, Be fruitful, and multiply, and replenish the earth, and subdue it: and have dominion over the fish of the sea, and over the fowl of the air, and over every living thing that moveth upon the earth." – **Genesis 1:26-28**

As we can see, humankind was created in the image of God. But as we know, God is Spirit. So the equipment we use to dominion this colony called earth is principally spiritual in nature. That is why we can all be said to be created in the image of God. Spiritually we are all same, since there is no physical form in the spirit.

God went on to state in Genesis 2 that it was not good for the man to be alone. But how could he be considered alone when God was with him? After all, God looked at his creation and declared it was all good. Perhaps God was acknowledging that even though he was with man (spirit-to-spirit) and that all was good, there were certain needs the man would have that would require a separate physical form and companion. So in Genesis 2 God did a remarkable thing.

And the Lord God formed man of the dust of the ground, and breathed into his nostrils the breath of life; and man became a living soul. **–Genesis 2: 7**

So God formed a physical earth-suit out of clay. And he put the perfect spiritual man that he had just created into this earth-suit called a *body*, and the *soul* was born. For the first time man became a living *soul*.

The purpose of the earth-suit (*body*) was to facilitate some of the physical tasks man needed to do in the garden. It is hardly possible for a spirit to cut the grass. The real man was still the spirit man that was created in Genesis 1, but now he was residing in the earth-suit that was formed in Genesis 2.

So if we are to have dominion over the earth today, it will not be done by the physical earth-suit man. It will be done by the spiritual man who was given the mandate in the first place. The physical earth-suit was never given the mandate to have dominion.

Then suddenly Satan came, in form of serpent, to deceive the woman. And the man followed. That act of disobedience transferred the legal ownership (title deed) of the earth to Satan. From that day he became the ruler of the darkness of this world. Since then, the earth and all its riches and resources have been under the (legally obtained) spiritual control of the enemy. So any Christian who wishes to partake of this earth's riches and wealth will have to defeat Satan first.

The person equipped and empowered by God to have such authority to dominate and defeat Satan, however, is not the earth-suit man formed in Genesis 2. It is the spiritual man formed in Genesis 1 that God gave the command to in the first place.

Unfortunately, because we have been in the earth-suit for so long, many of us now assume it is the physical man who has been given dominion ("rulership") and authority over the earth. This has caused many failures, defeats and frustrations for believers. To have command today over a resource of any value, you must forcefully take it away from satanic control by means of spiritual warfare and the force of righteousness. Money always flows in the direction of spiritual power. Nothing else will do. So as useful as academic education is, it won't give the believer any real advantage in the marketplace unless there is spiritual authority to back it up.

My mission in this book is to show you the satanic operation behind every activity and sector of the marketplace. And then to show you how you can and must win the spiritual battle first, before your physical tools (such as education and degrees) can work. I will be revealing the secrets of the satanic hierarchy that governs the earth. We will be looking at the marketplace sector by sector, from the media world to education, government, finance and business. We'll look at the world of entertainment and family life. We'll even look at the religious sector.

By the grace of God I will be showing you which satanic principality is behind each sector. We will learn its strengths and weaknesses and how we can defeat the giants (principalities) and rise to the top in these areas of the marketplace. That is how we as Christians can strategically invade the marketplace and command wealth transfer to happen, as God declared.

Remember, you are a spiritual person who happens to live in a *body*. The real battle is between the spiritual you and the satanic principalities. Once the battle is won by the spiritual you, the physical you can just bring home the harvest.

In the last days the mountain of the Lord's temple will be established as the highest of the mountains; it will be exalted above the hills, and all nations will stream to it. Many peoples will come and say, "Come, let us go up to the mountain of the Lord, to the temple of the God of Jacob. He will teach us his ways, so that we may walk in his paths." The law will go out from Zion, the word of the Lord from Jerusalem. He will judge between the nations and will settle disputes for many peoples. They will beat their swords into ploughshares and their spears into pruning hooks. Nation will not take up sword against nation, nor will they train for war any more. Come, descendants of Jacob, let us walk in the light of the Lord. **–Isaiah 2:2-5, NIV**

The purpose of wealth transfer is to extend the frontiers of God's kingdom, to give him tabernacles (*bodies*) to dwell in. So we must understand God's purpose for wealth before we can receive it and then glorify him with it. The point is to accomplish God's purpose on earth. It must never be about a personal empire —

otherwise Satan will have us for breakfast. We will have the backing and protection of heaven when our purpose is heaven-driven.

In the early days of my engagement with the marketplace as a Christian, I had a shallow sense of right and wrong and a misguided strategy. (My mantra was, the end justifies the means.) Over the years, God began to take me through painful acts of brokenness, emptying me of anything that Mammon could use for its purpose.

God began to show me that results can be misleading. If you look hard enough you will see the devil knows how to open doors too. He is a specialist in fattening the cows before killing them. So he bestows results on his own followers too, before utterly destroying them. It goes without saying that if the unjust do not store up, there will be nothing to transfer. So don't envy the ungodly.

A few months after I started this book project, someone heard me referring to its message in one of my teachings, and sent me a book by Johnny Enlow. I was thrilled to read it as it confirmed much of what God had been saying to me. When God starts a move, it spreads like wildfire. I suggest you get a copy of Enlow's book if you can. It will help to reinforce in your heart the message of this book, and we can never have too much knowledge.

The Bible says in Isaiah 33:6 *Wisdom and knowledge will be the stability of your times, and the strength of salvation. The fear of the LORD is his treasure."*

This means the strength of our salvation is determined by our knowledge of the realities of our redemption and our ability to manifest God's wisdom in all areas of life. We need to know who we really are before we can actualise who we're supposed to be. In the midst of the confusion this world is going through, we need an anchor — Jesus Christ, King of kings and Lord of lords. Join me today as we catch the electricity of the moment and bring God's glory to our door. In this way we can become all that God wants us to be.

This book is divided into two parts: A and B. Most Christian books that I have seen on this topic tend to focus only on effective marketplace strategies. These are good. But the Holy Spirit told me it was futile to teach technical war strategies to untrained fighters. We must first have a level of spiritual fitness and the capacity to implement any battle strategy.

In this book we'll start in Part A by looking at the

kind of person we need to be. In Part B we'll get into the breakthrough strategies. If we are not fit for battle, any description of the strategies would be a waste of time. In the marketplace we must *become* before we can *behold.*

So read Part A first. In the last days, Satan's counterfeit-making machine will be so improved that if possible even the Elect will be deceived. (Read Matthew 24:23-25). This is because for every good tree God has planted, Satan has planted counterfeits that look the same to the casual observer. So the leading of the Holy Spirit is the most vital tool for marketplace victory. But we cannot develop the required level of sensitivity to the Spirit of God if we do not renew our *mind.*

I have explained this principle in detail in Part A. It is only after we have been equipped and prepared in Part A that the strategies in Part B will make sense to us and become achievable.

Finally, this book is about the need for Christians to become Kingdom-minded. God's agenda goes beyond the happenings in our local church. It's about cities and nations. We all need to lift our gaze and see what God sees. This requires a level of maturity that is lacking in believers who are still entangling themselves in petty issues in the local church while the nations long to see the true children of God.

So increase your capacity, lift your game, refire your passion for God, and let us take this journey together. We will have a wonderful ride as we examine the secrets of dominion and breakthrough in the secular arena. Join me as we look into the perfect law of liberty, into who we are, what we have, what we can do and where we are going.

This book will transform your life. That is a guarantee. God bless you.

Charles Omole,
December 2013

PART A

The Making of the Soldier.

You cannot put new wine into an old wineskin. In the same way; you cannot implement a new pattern if the pattern is not birthed in you first. So to be able to reclaim the marketplace you need to be a prepared vessel. For this to happen you need to have grown where it matters, that is, in the Spirit.

You need to have a renewed and matured mind; yielded to the Spirit of God, to be an effective tool in his hands as we strategically invade the marketplace.

Part A of this book shows you how you can become a renewed and prepared weapon in God's hands, as you see the kingdoms of this world become the kingdoms of our God and of his Christ....Praise God.

Charles Omole

CHAPTER 1

THE RULER OF THIS WORLD'S DARKNESS

God had a perfect plan for us at creation. But as I stated earlier, humankind messed up that agenda. I also explained what that meant for dominion over the earth. The power of the cross is available to us so we can defeat the strongman and take over the marketplace. But to unbelievers, Satan still rules the earth and has full control over them.

So how does the earth operate today, under the dominion of Satan and his principalities? Let us begin our journey into biblical discovery.

Then the seventh angel sounded: And there were loud voices in heaven, saying, "The kingdoms of this world have become the kingdoms of our Lord and of His Christ, and He shall reign forever and ever!" **–Rev 11:15**

"And it shall come to pass in the last days, that the mountain of the Lord's house shall be established in the top of the mountains, and shall be exalted above the hills; and all nations shall flow unto it. And many people shall go and say, Come ye, and let us go up to the mountain of the Lord, to the house of the God of Jacob; and he will teach us of his ways, and we will walk in his paths: for out of Zion shall go forth the law, and the word of the Lord from Jerusalem." **–Isaiah 2: 2-4**

A closer look at these two scriptures reveals some fundamental realities that will affect all believers in these last days. First, the Bible says the kingdoms of this world will become the kingdoms of our Lord and of his Christ. This means there will be a kingdom collision. One kingdom is going to absorb another. This could be called a wealth transfer, that is; what is currently being controlled by the enemy will be transferred. So we know there will be a kingdom takeover.

How is it going to happen? Isaiah 2 says:
And it shall come to pass in the last days that the mountain of God's house shall be exalted above all mountains.

This means the Lord's mountain will be exalted above all others. This is important. Scripture tells us that the people who are not of the Lord will say: "Let us all go into the house of the Lord that they may teach us their ways."

That means the kingdom takeover will not be imposed by force alone. People will be persuaded by what they see. They will want to submit after seeing the excellence and superiority with which the Church is operating. Remember when the Queen of Sheba went to see Solomon?

The Bible says she entered Solomon's house, saw the orderliness of the house, saw the gold cutlery, and was so mesmerized by what she saw that her legs could no longer carry her. In other words, when she saw what Solomon had, even she, who came from an excellent background, had to acknowledge that this brilliance surpassed it.

So there is a certain transfer of wealth that will happen when the church develops certain strategies and values that others will envy. They will look at these and say, "Wow! I want what they have!"

This is what the Bible is saying in Isaiah, chapter two:

And they will say of their own free will, let us go into the house of the Lord, that they may teach us their ways (not their doctrines).

For this to happen, however, we need to understand the worth of what we carry as children of God. This is a challenge for the church generally. Many in the church do not fully understand the value of what they have received in Christ.

TYRE AND SIDON

We cannot talk about these issues in depth without first understanding the spiritual principle of Tyre and Sidon. In Ezekiel 27, the whole chapter is dedicated to these two cities. The Bible makes it clear in chapters 26 and 27 that there is no kind of trade or business that you won't find in Tyre and Sidon. They come to represent the commercial sphere. Whoever controls Tyre and Sidon controls the marketplace. And whoever controls the marketplace controls the destiny of nations.

In chapter 28 God tells Ezekiel to do two things — to proclaim and to lament. The first proclamation is against the *prince* of Tyre (from Ezekiel 28:1). From verse 11 he is to make a lamentation against the *king* of Tyre. We need to understand the difference between these two personalities (the prince and the king) so we can begin to decode the spiritual operations of the marketplace.

¹*The word of the Lord came to me again, saying,* ² *"Son of man, say to the prince of Tyre, 'Thus says the Lord God: "Because your heart is lifted up, and you say, 'I am a god, I sit in the seat of gods, in the midst of the seas,' yet you are a man, and not a god, though you set your heart as the heart of a god*³ *(Behold, you are wiser than Daniel!) there is no secret that can be hidden from you!* ⁴ *With your wisdom and your understanding you have gained riches for yourself, and gathered gold and silver into your treasuries;* ⁵ *by your great wisdom in trade you have increased your riches, and your heart is lifted up because of your riches),"*
⁶ *'Therefore thus says the Lord God: "Because you have set your heart as the heart of a god,* ⁷ *Behold, therefore, I will bring strangers against you, the most terrible of the nations; and they shall draw their swords against the beauty of your wisdom, and defile your splendour.* ⁸ *They shall throw you down into the Pit, and you shall die the death of the slain in the midst of the seas.*
⁹ *"Will you still say before him who slays you, 'I am a god'? But you shall be a man, and not a god, in the hand of him who slays you* .¹⁰ *You shall die the death of the uncircumcised*

by the hand of aliens; For I have spoken," says the Lord God."'
–Ezekiel 28:1-10 NKJV

When looking at the twin cities of Tyre and Sidon, we need to understand the principles involved. From verse 1 of Ezekiel 28, the Bible tells us that the word of the Lord came to Ezekiel saying, *"Son of man, say to the prince of Tyre, 'Thus says the Lord God: "Because your heart is lifted up, and you say, 'I am a god, I sit in the seat of gods, in the midst of the seas,' yet you are a man, and not a god...,*

This tells us the prince of Tyre is a human being like you and me. We can also see this up to verse 10 of the above chapter. The prince of Tyre is somebody we can see face to face.

After he made that declaration, God told him (verse 11) that he must now make a lamentation against the *king* of Tyre. As in any kingdom, the king is the real decision maker, with ultimate power. The prince can only function to the extent that the king delegates power to him. So who is this king of Tyre who spiritually controls the marketplace?

[11] Moreover the word of the Lord came to me, saying, [12]"Son of man, take up a lamentation for the king of Tyre, and say to him, 'Thus says the

Lord God: "You were the seal of perfection, full of wisdom and perfect in beauty. ¹³ You were in Eden, the garden of God; every precious stone was your covering: the sardius, topaz, and diamond, beryl, onyx, and jasper, sapphire, turquoise, and emerald with gold. The workmanship of your timbrels and pipes was prepared for you on the day you were created.

¹⁴ "You were the anointed cherub who covers; I established you; you were on the holy mountain of God; You walked back and forth in the midst of fiery stones.

¹⁵ You were perfect in your ways from the day you were created, till iniquity was found in you.

¹⁶ "By the abundance of your trading you became filled with violence within, and you sinned. Therefore I cast you as a profane thing out of the mountain of God; and I destroyed you, O covering cherub, from the midst of the fiery stones.

¹⁷ "Your heart was lifted up because of your beauty; You corrupted your wisdom for the sake of your splendour; I cast you to the ground, I laid you before kings, that they might gaze at you.

¹⁸ You defiled your sanctuaries by the multitude of your iniquities, by the iniquity of your trading. Therefore I brought fire from your midst. It devoured you, and I turned you to ashes upon the earth in the sight of all who saw you. ¹⁹All who knew you among the peoples are astonished at you; you have become a horror,

and shall be no more forever."""
–Ezekiel 28:11-19 NKJV

Remember, verses 1 to 10 were about the *prince* of Tyre. But verse 11 introduces the *king* of Tyre. The Bible states in verses 13-15:
"You were the seal of perfection, full of wisdom and perfect in beauty. You were in Eden, the garden of God; Every precious stone was your covering: the sardius, topaz, and diamond, beryl, onyx, and jasper, sapphire, turquoise, and emerald with gold. The workmanship of your timbrels and pipes was prepared for you on the day you were created. You were the anointed cherub who covers. I established you. You were on the holy mountain of God. You were perfect in your ways from the day you were created, till iniquity was found in you."

So who is the king of Tyre? It is *Satan*!

The *prince* of Tyre is a human being whom you can see face to face. He is anyone who is not born-again but who operates in the marketplace. Nature abhors a vacuum, so if you are not under the influence of God you must be under the influence of Satan. Hence, anyone you meet in your day to day activities, your boss, your business partner, your colleague — anyone in your workplace that you see around—all are princes of Tyre if they are not born again.

The real controller of the marketplace, however, is the *king* of Tyre. The prince is just a human being who is being used as a vessel to execute the king's desires. Why? Because when God created the earth, he declared that the only person who could operate legally in it was somebody born of a woman. Satan knows that. He knows he cannot operate freely without human helpers (princes). So demons rarely operate on earth outside the human vessels they occupy to carry out their wishes.

Satan influences people, then, and he uses people to achieve his objectives. The prince is a physical ruler over Tyre and Sidon (the marketplace) and the king, Satan, is its spiritual ruler. The physical ruler is the one we see, but the spiritual ruler is the one pressing the unseen buttons. So we know the physical ruler is not really our enemy. It is the spiritual ruler who is our enemy. When there is an issue, rather than struggling with the physical ruler, we need to go to where it matters and dislodge the spiritual ruler. Then the physical ruler suddenly becomes easy to deal with.

You see, we are not wrestling against flesh and blood. The people who are opposing us in the marketplace are not doing this by themselves, but under the influence of the king of Tyre. That king is using them to oppose us by proxy. So if we now descend into physical fighting, we've missed the point altogether. It is not about somebody's dislike of us, or opposition to us. The issue is, who is controlling that person? Until we understand the spiritual warfare going on in the marketplace, we will not succeed.

A typical example is a situation I had many years ago. I had just come back from a trip to the US and my wife gave me a piece of paper. On it she had written a petition complaining that her boss at work was making her life hellish. She believed it was racially motivated and so she had written a petition which she wanted me to proofread. I knew instantly this was not the way to handle the situation.

So we sat down and I explained Ezekiel 28 to her. If she wrote a petition, who was she going to give it to? She said their overall boss. I thought to myself: *You are trying to force change on a prince of Tyre, and you are giving another prince of Tyre the opportunity to adjudicate.*

What type of judgment would she get? I told her we had to deal with this situation differently. I asked her for the name of her manager at work, and I took the case to the throne room of God.

About a week later she came back from the office. "Guess what happened?" she said, excitedly. She told me their overall boss had come to their office and told her manager (the one giving the stress) that there was a position in another division and that he (the overall boss) had already volunteered this manager for that assignment. My wife's troublesome manager insisted she had not applied for a transfer, but the overall boss said he had already applied on her behalf and she was to start in the new division that same week. That day was the day the woman stopped being my wife's manager.

I then asked my wife, "How long did you think your petition would have taken to obtain a positive outcome?" She was ecstatic, and it was the end of her problem at work.

I had dealt with the issue where it mattered, rather than resorting to fleshly means. Sadly, many believers begin to fight and struggle, and as they are fighting in the flesh, they are fighting with the weapons the enemy controls. But if we fight through divine means, Satan does not know what to do with us.

It is important for us to understand that when people are opposing us physically, it is not about them. The devil will not physically oppose us, because he is not allowed to. Why?

Because the Lord has pronounced it so. Only a person born of a woman can legally operate here on earth. So the enemy must always operate through people and other proxies.

The truth is, if we are doing menial jobs or at the lower end of corporate ladder, or just starting a small business that has next to zero growth possibility, the enemy probably won't trouble us a lot (although we will still have our battles to fight). But as we begin to advance in the marketplace, we begin to encounter more resistance in all sorts of ways. We need to know how to deal with them, because if we deal with them in the flesh, we will never win. Our battle is primarily spiritual. The marketplace is a spiritual entity which we cannot dip into lightly.

I once read that the rate of business failure is highest in the Christian community. Why? It is partly because believers tend to be more trusting in an untrustworthy business climate. But mainly it is because our people stumble into business thinking it's about a business plan, some academic qualification, and a formula they have read about. They soon realize it is not that easy, and Satan will make sure of that. We must know that once we are a child of God, Satan has our number. It is not in his interest to make life easy for us.

The Bible says in Hebrews 11:29: *By faith they passed through the Red Sea as by dry land, whereas the Egyptians, attempting to do so, were drowned.*

This means there is a technology that God reveals to his own people, but it's one that works only on the platform of relationship. So if those who see what we do try to copy it exactly, it will not work for them.

Why is this? It is because they don't have relationship that will create the platform or the grace for that thing to work from. It works with the enemy in the same way. He will make certain things in the marketplace easier for his own people but will raise strong opposition against the child of God. Hence the need for spiritual warfare.

You observe an unbeliever who has done something wrong for ten years and never been caught. So you decide to do same. But do it once and you are caught! Satan will use every tool he has to fight a believer. We have an enemy who doesn't know the meaning of ceasefire. Why are many believers the most qualified in their workplace but often the lowest paid? Their bosses don't have a tenth of their qualifications.

We cannot fight the battle to reclaim the marketplace using the weapons controlled by the enemy, because for every educational certificate we bring to the marketplace, the enemy will bring five more people with better certificates.

So we can't win on that basis. We put the best business plan together and we don't get the funds. Then somebody walks in without any business plan and gets the money.

Remember what the Bible says about the battle not going to the strong? The favour of God is what distinguishes us. So as we consider how the marketplace operates, we must begin to fine-tune our strategies as believers.

Note here your Key Learning Points from Chapter 1

CHAPTER 2

NEW MIND NEEDED FOR NEW BATTLE

Understanding your spiritual make-up.
To be able to have dominion or a breakthrough in the marketplace, we need to be directed by the Holy Spirit. God has to be able to speak into our spirit, but this is usually not the problem. The difficulty is for our mind to be able to interpret what our spirit has picked up.

If we can hear from heaven, the earth must hear us. Our triumph in life is built on the voice of God (*rhema*) not just on hearing the Word of God, although one can aid the other. The faith of many people is weak today because they hear the Word of God all the time but they never hear from God.

Rhema is key to a breakthrough in the marketplace. Hearing the Word can help you to hear from God, but the two are not the same. So while you are hearing the Word, focus on hearing from God — *rhema*. Hearing from God, and not just hearing the Word, is what strengthens our faith. Nobody hears from God and doubts him. What distinguished the prophets of old was their ability to hear from God directly.

God does not communicate with the human mind or soul, however. He communicates only with the human spirit, as he did from the beginning. (Genesis 1:26-28.) Remember, the command to have dominion was given to the spirit-man, not the earth-suit man, as I explained in the Introduction.

Therefore we must possess a renewed (developed) mind to be able to actualise in the natural what God has instructed in the spiritual. This is so crucial as we engage in the marketplace. We have to know what battles to fight and how to fight, when we are engaging these economic and societal principalities.

We know clearly from 1 Thessalonians 5:23 that man is a spirit, he has a soul, and he lives in a body: *"Now may the God of peace himself sanctify you completely; and may your whole spirit, soul, and body be preserved blameless at the coming of our Lord Jesus Christ".*

In Genesis 1:26 the Bible says God created man in his image and after his likeness. And in Genesis 2:7 we saw that God formed man out of the dust of the earth. The man that God formed in Genesis 2 was just the physical body. The man that God created in Genesis 1 is the real man.

He is the spiritual entity with the likeness to God. So when God formed man in Genesis 2, he put the spirit which he had earlier created inside that body, and when the two came together, the soul was formed. Thus the soul of man is a combination of spirit and body.

Whether you are a believer or not, you still have three parts to you. You have the spirit, the body, and then between the two you have the soul. This is the tripartite combination of every person. The difference for unbelievers is that their spirit is dead to God but is alive to the spirit world of the devil.

Do not take this as a gruesome picture of all unbelievers congregating to worship the devil. But the Bible does say that to whom we yield our body, we are slaves. As believers we are slaves to righteousness, while unbelievers are slaves to iniquity or lawlessness. The Bible says *strong meat* is for those who through use have had their *senses exercised*.

"For though by this time you ought to be teachers, you need someone to teach you again the first principles of the oracles of God; and you have come to need milk and not solid food. For everyone who partakes only of milk is unskilled in the word of righteousness, for he is a babe. But solid food belongs to those who are of full age, that is, those who by reason of use have their senses exercised to discern both good and evil".
—Hebrews 5:12-14 (NKJV)

We can be unbelievers and yet exercise our spirits in such a way that we are alive to the demonic spirit world. That is why witches, sorcerers and people of that ilk can look at us and tell us our secrets. Even though they are unbelievers, they have trained their human spirit to communicate better with the evil spirit world. Just as there are dormant unbelievers, there are also active unbelievers.

That means there are unbelievers whose spirits are not sensitive, who are not actively pursuing the evil world even though they have access to it. And then there are the ones who are actively pursuing it.

In the same way there are inactive believers

whose spirits may be alive to God but who are not pursuing him. Then there are active believers who are fervently pursuing God, and as they train their spirits they are able to get more information from him.

To sum up, we all have a spirit, soul and body, whether or not we are believers. The difference is that the spirit of a believer is alive to God. If we are unbelievers, our souls are so wrapped up with the body and its accoutrements that our spirits are practically neglected. Hence we tend to follow our own will and lustful desires.

With our body we relate to the physical world; with our spirit we relate to the spiritual world, and with our soul, we relate with the intellectual world in what is called *self-consciousness*. In Genesis chapter 2:7, the Bible says *man became a living soul*. I will explain this in detail later in the book.

In the Bible, sometimes the word *soul* is substituted for the word *life*. This means we are what our souls are. Even though we are believers, it is the information contained in our souls that defines who we are experientially. That is why wrong minds lead to wrong thoughts, wrong thoughts lead to wrong emotions, and wrong emotions lead to wrong living.

Our spirit cannot communicate directly with our body. Neither can our body communicate directly with our spirit. By this I mean the carnal values which the body represents cannot relate to the consecration of a renewed human spirit. So they both communicate and consolidate their desires via the soul.

The battleground for the future of humankind is in our minds. *If anyone is in Christ, there is a new creation; the old has gone, the new has come.* (2 Cor 5:17, NIV) What remains in us of the old lifestyle is our memory.

We can still become a slave to our old memory, even after we are saved. Whoever wins the soul battle wins control over our life. Our soul makes it possible for our spiritual values to impact our body and be maintained by it. It is important to understand this.

Every human being has a spirit which is separate from the Holy Spirit. The three functions of our spirit are:
- **Conscience**
- **Intuition**
- **Communion**

Proverbs 25:28, Hebrews 12:23, Zechariah 12:1 and Romans 8:16 are just some of the scriptures that prove we each have a spirit.

1 Corinthians 2:11 - *For who knows a person's thoughts except their own spirit within them? In the same way no one knows the thoughts of God except the Spirit of God.*

Clearly the scripture here distinguishes between the spirit of a person and the Spirit of God. They are separate entities.

The Conscience Function
Our conscience is the organ which distinguishes right from wrong. This is what makes it different. It is a spontaneous, direct judgment based on the spirit of God. Our conscience does not discern right from wrong based solely on our own knowledge. Sometimes we are faced with something we don't have the full knowledge of, but we still know it is wrong. That is our conscience speaking. It is a spontaneous action.

We may be about to do something that is legal on paper but condemned by our conscience. Abortion is legal, isn't it? But if we consider abortion, we will hear our conscience telling us not to do it. Since the natural human law says it's okay, we are not likely to refrain as result of any stored knowledge of wrong, but something inside us still tells us it's wrong.

We make so many decisions on a day to day

basis. This is a function of our conscience. It is not a product of stored knowledge, but a spontaneous judgement. The work of conscience is independent and it is direct. It does not bend to outside opinions. It is not influenced by your soul or your body. What evidence is there of conscience? If you do wrong it will raise its voice of conviction.

John 13:21 – *When Jesus had said this, he became troubled in spirit.*
That was his conscience making the communication with him.

Acts 17:16 – *Now, while Paul was waiting for them at Athens, his spirit was being stirred up within him.*
Again, that is the conscience at work. Our conscience is the discerner that distinguishes right from wrong.

2Cor. 2:13 - *I had no rest for my spirit, not finding Titus my brother; but taking my leave of them, I went on to Macedonia.*
And now for the second function of our human spirit:

The Intuition Function.
Intuition is the sensing organ of the human spirit. It involves a direct sensing, devoid of any outside influences. Whatever comes to us

without any help from the mind, emotions or volition comes intuitively. Our intuition is what communicates with the Spirit of God. Every bit of information we get in our spirit we get via our intuition. It is just that often we need our mind to be in the right position to interpret it.

Have you ever woken up in the morning and been moved in your spirit to pray for somebody? You don't know what is happening, you don't know the person's problem, but you just feel you need to pray for him or her.

What is happening in your spirit is that your intuition is picking up heaven's frequency. The Spirit of God is talking to your spirit but because your mind can't interpret that information yet, you don't know the details. So you obey. You pray. Maybe the next day you discover that the person was going through some difficulty at that time or some armed robbers were about to invade that person's house. You didn't know all that when you were praying, but your intuition got the input directly from the Spirit of God.

The Holy Spirit cannot, does not and will not communicate with our human mind. He can only communicate with our spirit. Our spirit relays that information to our mind which then interprets it. The revelation of God and the movement of the Holy Spirit are known to the believers only through their intuition. A believer needs to heed the voice of conscience and the teaching of intuition. Others may call it discernment, but it doesn't really matter. The important thing is to be aware of the function and not be bogged down with the designation.

Evidence for the intuition function is in the Bible:

Mark 2:8 - *Immediately Jesus, aware in His spirit that they were reasoning that way within themselves, said to them, "Why are you reasoning about these things in your hearts?*

John 11:33 - *When Jesus therefore saw her weeping, and the Jews who came with her also weeping, he was deeply moved in spirit and was troubled.*

Acts 18:5 - *When Silas and Timothy had come from Macedonia, Paul was compelled by the Spirit, and testified to the Jews that Jesus is the Christ.*

Acts 20:22 (AMP) - *And now, you see, I am going to Jerusalem, bound by the [Holy] Spirit and obligated and compelled by the [convictions of my own] spirit, not knowing what will befall me there.*

In Acts 20:22, Paul knew something was wrong.

The Holy Spirit has already told him that this journey was going to be difficult. His intuition had received the information but his mind had not fully interpreted it, so he did not know exactly what was waiting for him at his destination, other than the fact there would be trouble.

The Communion Function
Our soul is not able to worship God. The Lord cannot be apprehended by our thoughts, feelings or intentions. He can only be known directly in our spirits, in what the Bible calls "the inner man." True worship is first of all a spiritual connection with God.

Our spirit picks up signals and messages and our souls bring mental understanding of that signal. Deep calls to deep. The Spirit always communicates only with the spirit. God's Spirit cannot communicate with our soul. If he could, it would mean the moment we became saved our mind would be fully renewed as well.

When we become born again, our spirit gets renewed but our mind is as dead as it always was. So we have to go through a process the Bible calls the renewing of our mind (Romans 12:2). Our soul is something we work on continually until Jesus comes. You and I know that. The point is that the Holy Spirit always communicates with our spirit. The question is, can our spirit then translate that information to our soul?

For instance, why is it when we are around certain people, they get a word of knowledge about what is happening in our life? How can we explain it? In this example, the person's intuition picked up a signal from the Spirit of God and translated that information to his mind. His mind was then able to interpret that information and give it to you.

That is why many of us do not walk in the gifts of the Spirit even though we are praying for them. Usually the problem is not with our spirit connecting with the Spirit of God. The problem is with our mind being able to receive that information and interpret it.

Evidence of communion in the Bible:

John 4:23 – *But the hour is coming, and now is, when the true worshipers will worship the Father in spirit and truth; for such people the Father seeks to be his worshipers.*

Romans 7:6 (KJV) – *We serve….in the new life of the spirit".*

Romans 8:16 – *"The Spirit himself bears*

witness with our spirit that we are children of God".

Romans 1:9 - *For God, whom I serve in my spirit in the preaching of the gospel of his Son, is my witness as to how unceasingly I make mention of you…*

1 Corinthians 6:17 (AMP) - *But the person who is united to the Lord becomes one spirit with him.*

Sometimes the word communion is used for the words *serve, sing,* and *united.* It also means *fellowship.*

So these are the three functions of the human spirit which work together in a coordinated fashion. Our conscience judges right from wrong but this is not based on stored knowledge because it is not the same as the mind. Our conscience judges right from wrong based on intuition, just as the Spirit bears witness with our spirit that we are a child of God.

A good example is smoking. We never find it written anywhere in the Bible that smoking is a sin. But we do know that our body is the temple of the Holy Spirit. If our body is the temple, do we then destroy that temple deliberately? Many people still smoke after they get saved. This doesn't mean they are not saved. But we find that after a while they stop smoking. If we were to ask them why, they would tell us that something in their spirit just told them enough was enough.

What happened there? It was not our telling them to stop. They stopped because their conscience began to worry them about it, based on intuition. Intuition picked up the signal from heaven saying, "Stop smoking!" Then intuition told conscience and conscience said, "Stop smoking."

Intuition is sometimes like a nagging child. It just won't go away until we yield. Sometimes intuition pesters us like that: *Stop smoking, stop smoking.* It gets to the point where we just can't ignore it. But this voice is a gentle; it doesn't slap us around. Conscience judges according to intuition. Intuition is related to communion or worship in that God is known by us intuitively. Let me put it this way – the human mind does not have the capacity to know God or relate to him.

Think about it. If we are honest with ourselves, sometimes we wake up and ask ourselves, *Is there a God?* Sometimes we see something and ask, *Is there a God?* Sometimes our mind becomes so blown away that we lack the capacity even to understand the concept of God, much less find him. The only way we can know God is in our spirit.

Intuitively we know God exists. If someone says prove it, we can't prove it. But we know. That kind of knowing is a spirit knowing, not a mind knowing. Mind knowing tends to be based on proof, but spirit knowing is just knowing, period. If somebody says, "Are you saved? How do you know?" There is nothing we can say to prove it other than we just know. So it is important to understand that God can be known only in our spirit and not in our mind.

The problem many believers have is that when we get saved, we forget we need to develop our human spirit so we can effectively relate to the Spirit of God. That is why the Bible says strong meat is for those who by reason of use have their senses exercised.

Our spirit has a real function in our ability to be able to relate with God. In terms of our ability to relate with God with our spirit, it is not difficult. In fact it is usually automatic. The Spirit of God just does it. The real battle ground is our mind. Let me put it this way: If God wants to talk to us, he talks to our human spirit. Our spirit relays this to our mind, and our mind makes us aware of it by interpreting it and bringing recognition.

If we have a mind that is polluted and unrenewed, always short-circuiting the flow, we'll find that whenever God speaks, everything ends in our human spirit. It never gets relayed to our soul. If we continue like this for a long time, we reach a point where we desensitise our soul completely. Our ability to pick up signals from God becomes weaker and weaker. Once that happens we become a slave to the flesh.

There is no way we can be a spiritually sensitive child of God, and then sin and not know it. If we are not aware of sin knowledge-wise, our conscience will tell us it is wrong by intuition. Many of us know this to be true.

That is the job of the conscience. Even when we don't know scripturally that something is wrong, if we are sensitive, our conscience will inform us. Its ability to tell us right from wrong has nothing to do with how much we know – it is a direct input from the Spirit of God.

Note here your Key Learning Points from Chapter 2

CHAPTER 3
UNDERSTANDING AND DEVELOPING A NEW MIND FOR THE MARKETPLACE BATTLE

Understanding the Operations of Human Soul

Let us now look at the human soul. We are what our soul is. The elements which make us human belong to the soul. Intellect, thought, ideals, emotions, love, choice, decision and discernment are all experiences of the soul. This is why the Bible sometimes calls a person a "soul," as though we only have this element. We see this in the following Scripture verses:

Genesis 12:5 (KJV) – *And Abram took Sarai his wife, and Lot his brother's son, and all their substance that they had gathered, and <u>the souls that they had gotten</u> in Haran; and they went forth to go into the land of Canaan; and into the land of Canaan they came.*

Genesis 46:27 – *"And the sons of Joseph, which were born him in Egypt, were <u>two souls: all the souls of the house of Jacob</u>, which came into Egypt, were threescore and ten.*

The seat and essence of human personality is the soul. But the soul has three main faculties which work hand in hand:
- **Mind**
- **Volition**
- **Emotion**

Our **mind** is the instrument of our thought and intellect, the seat of our intellectual power. From the mind we have wisdom, knowledge and reasoning.

Psalm 139:14 - *I will give thanks to You, for I am* fearfully and wonderfully made; Wonderful are Your works, and my soul knows it very well.*

Lamentations 3:20 - *Surely my soul remembers and is bowed down within me.*

Proverbs 24:14 - *Know that wisdom is thus for your soul; If you find it, then here will be a future, and your hope will not be cut off.*

Our **volition** is our will, our power to choose. Volition is the instrument for our decisions, whether willing or unwilling. Without volition, we would be reduced to robots and zombies. Volition at work exposes the wisdom or foolishness of human decisions.

Psalm 27:12 – *Deliver me not over unto the will (original word is soul) of mine enemies....*

Job 7:15 - *... my soul would choose suffocation and death rather than my pain.*

Our **emotions** are our feelings. Love, hate, joy, anger, sadness, happiness and other feelings are all included. Emotions can be seen in affection, desire and sensing.

1Samuel 18:1 - *Now it came about when he had finished speaking to Saul that the soul of Jonathan was knit to the soul of David, and Jonathan loved him as himself.*

Deuteronomy 6:5 - *You shall love the LORD your God with all your heart and with all your soul and with all your might.*

Psalms 42:5 - *Why are you in despair, O my soul? And why have you become disturbed within me? Hope in God, for I shall again praise Him for the help of His presence.*

2 Peter 2:8 - *For by what he saw and heard, that righteous man [Lot] while living among* them, felt his righteous soul tormented day after day by their lawless deeds.*

THE HEALTHY MIND

Romans 12:1-3 — *I beseech you therefore, brethren, by the mercies of God, that you present your bodies a living sacrifice, holy, acceptable to God, which is your reasonable service. ² And do not be conformed to this world, but be transformed by the renewing of your mind, that you may prove what is that good and acceptable and perfect will of God.*

Note the need for our minds to be renewed.

Proverbs 23:7 – *For as he thinks in his heart, so is he. "Eat and drink!" he says to you, but his heart is not with you.*

For a believer, a healthy mind is not an option. It is a necessity. Because our mind informs our actions and inclinations, the quality of those actions is basically determined by the quality of our mind.

Every action of our lives is first conceived in our mind. So it is foolish to assume that because we are thinking of something but not doing it, it is not dangerous. Let me put it this way: every single thought that is conceived in our mind is a step away from actually being performed by us.

We cannot act out what we have not thought of. If somebody suddenly comes to us and suggests a lesbian or gay relationship, the only reason we can emphatically say it is impossible is that we have never thought of it.

It is impossible to be tempted or led astray in an area in which we have never sown a thought in the past. The problem many of us have is that our mind is a ticking time bomb of bad thoughts waiting to be manifested if we don't deal with them.

We may not be acting it out yet, but are we already thinking of sleeping with other people? Are we already thinking of taking somebody else's wife or husband? Are we already thinking of stealing money? Okay, we have not done any of them yet, but everything is already taking place in our mind. We may be a few steps away from disaster because our thoughts control our actions and inclinations.

Inclination does not necessarily reflect something we have done. But it reflects what we most likely would do, given the right set of circumstances. So it is important for us to discipline our thoughts. One way I personally deal with the issue is that whenever a thought comes to my mind, the first thing I ask myself is: *is this a thought I want to see manifested as an action?* If the answer is no, I reject it immediately. The longer a thought lingers in our mind, the greater the power it has over us.

The Bible tells us to speak with the enemy in the gate. That is the entrance. We don't speak with the enemy in our bedroom. By the time he is in our bedroom, he has come through the gate, through our courtyard, and through our living room. So we have already grown into it over a period of time and are now trying to reject it at the last moment. By this time the thought says *I'm not going anywhere!* It is much harder to get rid of such a thought because it has put down a root inside us.

Some of these thoughts are rather funny. I remember being on a Singapore Airlines flight from the Philippines to Singapore. I couldn't believe the airport security in the Philippines! When you get to the airport your main luggage is x-rayed before you even take it in. Normally passengers don't see how their main luggage is x-rayed as this is done after you have checked in. But in the Philippines, it has to be x-rayed and stamped before check-in.

Then the hand luggage goes through the x-ray. After immigration there is still another x-ray. (By now your hand luggage has been x-rayed twice.) Then before you board the aircraft they open every bit of hand luggage. I started thinking, even with all this security, what if there were some terrorists on board? Then I thought, if the plane were to be blown up, what would happen to me?

Then I said to myself, *Hold on a second, what are you thinking about? Reject the thought immediately!* So I did so immediately and focused my mind on more edifying matters.

Our mind can indeed play games! It is a creative force. Or our children go on a school trip and maybe we remember some children who died during a similar trip and our mind dwells on the disaster. We had better reject that thought immediately so you don't sow the seed of an actual calamity.

What we call "worry" is actually a seed being sown in our soul. Have you ever worried about something and it came to pass? That is exactly the problem. Because we worry about it, we are setting the stage for it to happen. So don't think anything that is just happening in your mind is innocent.

We can know the quality of a person's mind from the quality of their actions. We have not yet failed but we have thought of failing a million times. We can create wrong emotions in our life through wrong thoughts. Perhaps crime figures are low, but the moment we hear the news of one or two murders something in our mind goes into panic mode.

In 2002, in the UK, two schoolgirls called Holly and Jessica were abducted and murdered. As a result, thousands of parents expressed an interest in signing up for an untested and experimental procedure to implant microchips in the backs of their children's hands. The idea was, if a child went missing, the chip could be activated and a satellite could locate the child. It did not occur to these well-meaning parents that a crazy person could simply just sever the hand. Many parents now want a chip to ensure their children's safety, despite uncertainties about the chip's effects.

We are a hundred times more likely to be killed by a drunken driver than to be kidnapped and killed. But people ignore these statistics. Abductions like the above are rare, but because they make national headlines, we think they happen often. What leads to a high fear of crime when there is actually no crime? Our minds.

Then our mind (thoughts) informs our mood. Maybe as we begin to think about the good old days when we first met our spouse, we find ourselves smiling. Then people wonder what is happening to us! Or when we think of sad events in our life, maybe the death of a loved one, we immediately find ourselves becoming moody.

Thoughts and emotions
Our thoughts inform our emotions, and no bad thoughts are harmless. They inform our disposition. The rule with every negative thought that comes our way is to see ourselves actually doing it, because that may be a step away from happening. So if we don't want to do it, we don't think about it. This is important because the moment we begin to think about something negative, it begins to weaken our defences, and before we know it, we are acting it out.

This is what Jesus meant when he was talking about adultery and fornication. He said if we have thought about it, we have done it. There are those who have physically committed it, and there are those who are thinking about it. Jesus says both are guilty.

Why does he say that? He knows that the moment we think about it, it becomes possible for us. Do we ever sit down and think about killing our loving mother? I may sound a bit dramatic here, but of course we don't think about things like that. We know nothing would ever bring us that disposition. I've used that shocking example to show that we only think about things we are inclined to perform. If it is something we would never find ourselves doing, we would be able to effortlessly bounce the thought out of our mind.

Please understand: Every negative thing we think about lets the devil know what he can get us with. It reveals our potential weak spots. It is as if the United States and Russia were fighting and Russia announced its east flank was weak, as well as its north-west flank. By announcing its weak places, Russia suggests to the USA the best places to penetrate. Well, you might say, *that's a stupid way to fight a battle!* But that is exactly what we do with our minds.

Every day we announce to the devil, "Don't bother bringing homosexual temptations my way; just bring money temptations to me instead! Don't bother bringing fornication my way; bring this theft idea my way instead." When we declare our potential inclinations to the devil, we let him know how he might attack us.

Often our happiness or sadness is a product of our thoughts. If we often sit down and think about our financial difficulties, doesn't it make us moody? A day later we may be at a friend's birthday party. But although our financial situation hasn't changed, we don't bother thinking about it and are just as jolly as everybody else.

FEAR (False Evidence Appearing Real) is an emotion. Whose report will you believe? I choose to believe the report of the Lord. It is possible to be afraid when there is nothing to be afraid of, simply because we are thinking wrongly. Our thoughts create situations for us. They create our world. What we think about may create fears within us which are not based in reality. It is even possible to think we are in love with someone when in fact we are not in relationship with that person.

Have you ever been in an office where a female or male colleague just happens to be a nice person who smiles at people? You may begin to think how it would be good to have whatever with him or her. In your mind you may conceive of an affair when in reality nothing is happening. That is what happens to stalkers, those people who harass celebrities, for instance.

A stalker may have never met the person face to face, but in his deranged mind he has visualised being married to and having children with that person. As a result he is mentally hooked to that celebrity even though the celebrity has no emotional hook with him. The stalker's mind has created a world as real as flesh and blood, simply because he has thought about it.

It happens in psychiatric cases, where a person's thoughts create his world and his realities. Our realities are a function of our thoughts.

Please don't sit down and allow all kinds of thoughts to creep into your mind. Because once that happens they begin to inform your actions and inclinations. We can never become what we have never perceived in our mind. That is why the saying goes, if you want to be a millionaire, think like a millionaire! It suggests that if we physically want to become a millionaire we must first picture it in our heart. Some people will see £100,000 stacked up and faint with shock! Yet they tell God, "I want to be a millionaire!"

A thought is a seed. And meditation on it makes it grow into your reality, as we see in Joshua 1:8.

This Book of the Law shall not depart from your mouth, but you shall meditate in it day and night, that you may observe to do according to all that is written in it. For then you will make your way prosperous, and then you will have good success.

It is only after we meditate on something that it can begin to impact our ways. This works both positively and negatively.

Wrong thoughts lead to wrong actions, inclinations and behaviour and wrong actions and inclinations lead to wrong living. We cannot live right if we are constantly thinking wrongly.

Understanding the mind game
We cannot think wrongly and still live right. The Bible says in Romans 12 that we should be transformed by the renewing of our minds. But this transformation can only happen if we meditate on the right things. I hope we have a greater appreciation of that scripture now. The Holy Spirit through our intuition and conscience may be assuring us of our safety in God, but at the same time our mind may be thinking of all the crime in our city. The two are not communicating on the same frequency.

When our mind cannot interpret what it is getting from our spirit, we go with the flow of our natural senses. What we think about matters. Before we do your exam we are already thinking of failure — perhaps because we have not fully studied the lessons. But even if we have studied and are ready for the exam, we can be sure that if we continue thinking of failure, we are a step away from the worst happening. We have got to be able to tell ourselves that nothing like that will happen.

That is why one of the characteristics of "successful" people is their apparent arrogance. The moment we stand confidently and say this is what is going to happen, people accuse us of arrogance. They would prefer to see in us a kind of false humility. But success has to do with the mental discipline of thinking in a certain way. This discipline enables us to follow the example of Joshua in the scripture just mentioned (1:8).

If somebody tells me I am a rich man and I answer, "Oh, I'm not really rich," that's nonsense. If you tell me I am a rich man, I'll tell you, "Yes, I'm twice as rich as you think!" Stop this silly humility. In my early days at university, after a particular exam somebody came to me and said, "You were brilliant in that exam and I'm sure you are going to get an 'A'."

I stupidly said, "Me? No way!" in an attempt to appear humble. On the one hand I was praying I would pass the exam, and on the other hand I was using my mouth to say I had not done well in it. That was silly humility.

If someone says you have done well in an exam, agree with them! That may sound arrogant because you are not displaying the false humility expected by the world. But you need to guard your heart with all diligence because out of it flow the issues of life.

In the early 1960s President J.F Kennedy stood up to make his State of the Union speech in the US Congress. He told the people that within ten years American would be on the moon. Prior to that time they had the means to be there but nobody had thought about it. The moment he announced that, and put resources behind it, suddenly it became a possibility in people's minds. And because it was mentally possible, it happened within ten years. Your thoughts matter a lot.

Philippians 4:8 - *Finally, brethren, whatever things are true, whatever things are noble, whatever things are just, whatever things are pure, whatever things are lovely, whatever things are of good report, if there is any virtue and if there is anything praiseworthy—meditate on these things.*

The Bible says God will do exceedingly abundantly above all we can ask or think. That means God responds to our thoughts in the same way he responds to our words. Now we understand why. He said more than we can ask *or* think. He didn't say *ask and think*. Part of the shallowness of some exponents of the faith movement is their assertion that you can "name it and claim it," regardless of what you are thinking about. What you think about *does* matter. Often in the Bible, Jesus could see what people were thinking in their hearts and would respond accordingly.

Matthew 9:4 - *And Jesus knowing their thoughts said, "Why are you thinking evil in your hearts?"*

Matthew 12:25 -*And knowing their thoughts, Jesus said to them, "Any kingdom divided against itself is laid waste; and any city or house divided against itself will not stand."*

Those people never said a word, but as they thought to themselves, *Who do you think you are?* Jesus picked it up. He knew what they were thinking and addressed it. In exactly the same way, God responds to your thoughts. You can say what you will, but what you are thinking in your heart matters just as much.

Today I want us to do an exercise to clear our mind of its baggage. When thoughts come to me of things I don't want to do, I reject them at once. I say, *In Jesus name, get out!* Sometimes

I say it aloud. Sometimes I say it inside, if I am in a crowded place, as I don't want people to think I'm mad. But the point is, the moment I do that, the thought disappears. Try it. It works one hundred percent of the time.

The moment a fresh thought comes our way that we don't like, we must reject it and it will go away instantly. And it will not come back for some time. When we have just started doing this, we might seem to be doing it every five minutes. We'll do it many times a day to clear our mind. After a while it happens less often because our mind is getting used to having only godly and edifying thoughts in it.

The cleaner our mind is, the better. So it is important to be able to receive the godly promptings from our intuition. Another example I give about the mind is when we are praying. The Bible says that when we are praying in the spirit, our understanding is unfruitful. This means we don't understand what we are saying. This is a greater reason to "will" our thoughts into submission — so we can pick up heaven's frequency.

If we are praying for the growth of the church, for example, the best thing is for our mind to begin to visualise that growth taking place. If God wants to drop into our spirit a strategy about how that should be achieved, he will do so because our mind is in sync with what we are praying about. So our mind can grasp that word and we can share it with the people.

When we are praying in the spirit for the growth of the church, some people, however, are cooking dinner in their minds. Our mind may be in the kitchen, or sorting out our agenda for tomorrow. It may be doing a million and one things apart from the real thing we are doing. Our prayer then becomes a monologue because we are not able to receive back. I know people who have cooked a three-course meal while taking part in a prayer meeting.

Some people are praying so much in the spirit that even when the prayer leader says Amen, in Jesus name, they are still praying because they are not there. They've gone. But in all things God is sovereign. He can do what only he can do, in the way that pleases him.

Holiness
The need for mind renewal is essential. Holiness is based on the moral decisions we make when we continually align our lives to the will and purposes of God. A renewed mind is a necessity for holy living. There is no way you can live in conformity with the Scriptures if your mind is full of anti-Scripture thoughts. Let me

put it this way: your mind is the pool from which your actions are taken.

Assume for one moment that you could take your mind out of your body, and put it where you could see it. Now every time you want to act physically or do something, your body looks at your mind (the pool, the resources) to decide its course of action. Your body looks at your mind, picks up a thought from there, and acts on it.

Your mind is like an action bank for your body. If you have thought about killing people, if you have thought about stealing, if you have thought about rape, even though you have not actually done these things, their turn to be acted upon will eventually come. One by one, the action will follow the thoughts if you don't get rid of them.

It is important for us to realise that what we put in our mind is crucial. That is why the process of renewal of the mind is so important. And what we will look at in the chapters that follow is how we can renew our minds. This is the nitty-gritty of the Christian faith. This is the foundation, what determines whether we stand or fall.

These days, many people have itchy ears. They would rather be in churches where they hear what they want to hear. They are not established in anything. And these are foundation issues.

The Formation of Christ in us

Why do we need a healthy mind? Why do we need to renew it? There are many reasons. In the next chapter I will explain five key exercises you can begin to do, to develop a healthy mind, both in terms of Scripture and in terms of practice. Have you ever met people to whom certain sins are completely alien? To some people, taking what does not belong to them is so alien that they don't understand why people do it.

I read about a guy who went to one of the shops on Oxford Street and bought a few things. He lived outside of London, and when he got home he noticed that one item out of about thirty had not been paid for. So he called around and found the shop did not have a branch in his area. So he drove all the way back to Oxford and returned to that shop.

The staff member he spoke to said, "Why did you bother?" She said he should have just taken it. He refused, and paid for it. When she asked him why, he just said he didn't have peace with any other course of action.

Some people do not go out with the intention of stealing anything, but in their mind they have already accommodated this sort of event. They say, "Well, it is a free gift from God," and they just keep it.

Why do we need renewed minds? It is because the body is the servant of the mind — whether it be carnal or spiritual. And each kind of mind produces its own fruit.

1. We need a healthy and renewed mind to present our bodies to God.
We are to present our bodies to God continually, as a living sacrifice.

Romans 12:1 - *I beseech you therefore, brethren, by the mercies of God, that you present your bodies a living sacrifice, holy, acceptable to God, which is your reasonable service.*

It is a **sacrifice** because it is dead to its own life; it is **holy** because it is consecrated to God, and it is **living** because Christ lives in us.

One reason why we need a healthy mind is so we can present our bodies to God as an acceptable, holy and living sacrifice. There is no way we can do this if our minds are not renewed. For our worship to be acceptable to

God, we must please him through our obedience to his instructions, obedience which is rooted in our minds. We are to continually present our physical bodies until this becomes a part of our spiritual service.

In 1 Corinthians 6:19, the Bible says our body is the temple of the Holy Spirit. This body must be presented in an acceptable way by the Holy Spirit so that we can be effective vessels for God to use. We know our body has an inclination towards the flesh and cannot be renewed. And yet the Holy Spirit can present it as acceptable to God if God can see that our mind has been cleared of any negative promptings that would make our body manifest its true nature.

While the flesh (carnal mind) cannot be destroyed in this physical body, it can be kept in check. And the only way we can keep it in check is when our mind is spiritual and not carnal. Think about it. If our spirit and body are trying to influence our mind and our mind is already full of negative thoughts, who is going to win that battle?

Our body will, of course. Because all those negative thoughts have already given our body the edge. It is important that we don't give the devil the raw material with which he can manifest his finished products in our lives. We need a healthy mind for that purpose.

Romans 6:16 – *Do you not know that to whom you present yourselves slaves to obey, you are that one's slaves whom you obey, whether of sin leading to death, or of obedience leading to righteousness?*

This is the crunch of the matter. With our voice we can proclaim we are serving God, but we are a slave to whomever we yield ourselves. So if we have yielded ourselves to the devil through accepting all kinds of evil thoughts, we are a slave to him even though we claim to be serving God. If our mind is already a slave to sin, there is no way we can serve God effectively. We have to keep sin out.

No matter how big a ship is, it is only able to keep afloat if it keeps the environment out of itself. The moment the environment (represented by water) begins to go inside that ship, it begins to sink no matter how big it is.

So our duty is to block these thoughts from our minds. They will still come because we are in the world. That is why the Bible says we do not war after the flesh but against the spiritual forces of evil. It also says we are in the world but not of the world.

So these thoughts will come, but our duty is to speak with our enemies in the gate, to arrest the thoughts the moment they arrive.

In the same way, when we are married, if at any time during a quarrel divorce comes into our mind, we are only a few steps from seeing this as a possibility. If divorce is completely excluded from our minds and from our dictionaries, however, no matter what situation we are facing, we know we will have to resolve it somehow because divorce is not an option. We must each guard our heart with all diligence for out of it flow the issues of life.

Friends, if we don't want to do certain things, it is time for us to stop thinking about those things. We are not permitted to think about what we don't want to do. That is the rule.

Some of you may be praying for certain things but God has not given them to you because you have not done the mind clearing exercise. If he were to bring those things your way right now, they would trigger certain negative, dormant thoughts in your heart, thoughts which would soon become manifest.

Suppose you have been thinking, *if I see money I will steal.* Meanwhile, you have been asking God to give you a well-paying job. God may have a job for you as a senior manager in a bank, but he says, *Hold on a second! This person has been thinking about stealing money (although he/she has not actually stolen it yet). If I give this person a senior job in a bank, am I not an accomplice to his disobedience?*

Your being in the bank would just trigger that thought. For now that it has been dormant because you have not had the means or the opportunity to express it. But the moment God gave you that job, it could happen much more easily.

You have to clear your mind in such a way that you can receive fresh blessings from God. Your mind can prevent you from receiving from God because you could possibly kill yourself with the things God gave you. In this book I am a postman, delivering a message. I know it is for you because your name is written on the envelope, but I don't know what it specifically applies to in your life.

I want you to think about this carefully. God cannot be mocked. If indeed we are to make ourselves different from everybody out there, it is time for us to begin to walk in the realities of Scripture. It is clear that our minds have the power to affect what happens to us.

In certain circumstances you may not be able to receive many things you are praying for until you have cleansed your mind of some dangerous and carnal thoughts that have taken roots in it. For instance, you may have been thinking about having sex all over the place and you are praying that God would give you a job in the leisure industry. God sees a job, maybe in a mostly-female leisure club as the manager.

God says, *Ah-ah! If I gave him that job it would trigger an action based on the adulterous thoughts he already has!* So a way to get that job may be to clear the mind of those thoughts first. The irony of this principle is that because our thoughts are our deepest secrets, not known by anybody else, we think we can let them go wild. Believe me, we cannot afford to, not if we want to walk with God.

The Bible tells us we wrestle not against flesh and blood but against principalities and against powers, against wicked spirits in heavenly places. It also tells us to bring every thought into captivity.

2 Corinthians 10:5 - *Casting down arguments and every high thing that exalts itself against the knowledge of God, bringing every thought into captivity to the obedience of Christ.*

Make sure, then that every thought you allow into your mind is in sync with the Holy Spirit. How do you know it is a right thought? That is easy. Your conscience will tell you and you will know instantly.

The moment a thought comes to you, ask yourself, would I want to be seen doing this? If the answer is no, you need to kill that thought immediately. Because if you allow it to continue, it will develop a stronghold over you. And before you know it, it will be hard to extinguish.

Let me put it this way: every time the devil wants to tempt you, he consults with your mind. He says, okay, what else can I throw his way, from his thoughts? He'll look for something you have already thought of and out of that he will pick up the next temptation and bring it your way.

2. We need a healthy and renewed mind to identify God's will.

With a renewed mind we can search out, identify and prove what the will of God is for our lives and the lives of others. Only a renewed mind can say that God's will is good. Only a renewed mind can accept God's will as a perfect choice in the process of decision making. Only a renewed mind can incubate and implement divine strategies. And in these last days, these are what we need. But divine strategies will not be revealed to those whose minds are not renewed.

The state of our soul is important if we want to identify what the will of God is. We live in a day and age when many of our decisions are no longer between actions that were traditionally considered to be either right or wrong. This simplistic way of looking at decisions becomes less and less helpful as we mature in God.

Should I steal or should I not steal? That scenario is so basic that it should not occupy the mind of a mature believer. As the end of the age draws near, we are going to be faced with situations where the decisions are between two choices that appear to be okay.

For instance, Natwest Bank UK, offers you a job. Almost immediately Barclays Bank UK also offer you a job. But only one of these is God's perfect will. So how do you know which job to take?

The moment we must choose between two things that are not necessarily evil, our decision-making runs into difficulty. This is where sensitivity comes in. How we discern the perfect will of God will depend on the state of our soul.

So we need to have healthy minds so we can cooperate maximally with the Holy Spirit without the destructive influence of the flesh.

3. We need a healthy and renewed mind to identify our self-image in Christ

We need a healthy mind to know who we are. A renewed mind allows us to develop a sound judgment of who we are in Christ and the realities of our redemption. A renewed mind allows us to think as God wants us to think. Let me put it this way: thinking lowly of yourself is a form of pride. So is thinking you are better than others. But to think highly of yourself *in Christ* is right.

When an object is the only one in the world, it is highly valued. You are unique and the only one of your kind. So think highly of yourself in Christ. Often we do not think highly enough of ourselves, preferring to compare ourselves with others. If we think of ourselves as God would want us to think of ourselves, that is the product of a renewed and balanced mind.

If we do not have renewed minds, failure or pride will dominate our lives. If we think too lowly of ourselves we deprive ourselves of the blessings of God. If we think too highly of ourselves, our heads become as big as the Tower of London but there is nothing to show for it.

We can never think of ourselves properly, the way God wants us to think, if we don't have renewed minds.

Romans 12:3 (AMP) - *For by the grace (unmerited favour of God) given to me I warn everyone among you not to estimate and think of himself more highly than he ought [not to have an exaggerated opinion of his own importance], but to rate his ability with sober judgment, each according to the degree of faith apportioned by God to him.*

An unhealthy self-image leads to unhealthy comparisons between Christians.

2 Corinthians 10:12 (AMP) - *Not that we [have the audacity to] venture to class or [even to] compare ourselves with some who exalt and furnish testimonials for themselves! However, when they measure themselves with themselves and compare themselves with one another, they are without understanding and behave unwisely.*

The Bible says we are foolish if we compare ourselves with other people. In any case we don't know what is going on inside them. So let's not do it.

Those who don't have a healthy image of themselves begin to compare their church with another church, compare themselves with other people, compare their business with another's business. They are constantly comparing. Why? Because they need to see us failing in order to feel comfortable with their own failure. Even some Christian leaders take joy in seeing other people fail because it somehow makes them look better. If we need the failure of somebody else to make us look better, we are failures ourselves.

If you have a healthy image of yourself you don't care what others think or do, because you are going on different journeys.

One of my mentors told me, Charles, *the only object that has all the parts of the body of equal size is a monster.* Every body you consider normal will have big parts, like the head. and small parts, like the little finger. The same goes for the church of God. Thank God there are churches like the head, which are massive, and churches like the tooth, which are small and hidden.

But we know that when our tooth aches the whole body feels it. A big church has benefits, a small church has benefits. It all depends on where you are with God, on what God wants to do in your life, and on the assignment he has given you.

We need to have a healthy self-image, because if we are sure of who we are, then the news that others are doing well makes us give glory to God. We are not threatened by anybody because we know who we are in Christ Jesus.

If God put only you on the face of this earth, you would thrive. That is how you need to understand yourself. And you cannot have that mindset if your mind is not renewed.

4. We need a healthy and renewed mind to perceive what God has prepared for us in life and the marketplace

Only the renewed mind can perceive what God has prepared. Strategies to overcome principalities are known to God, and they can be yours if your mind is renewed and able to interpret what God is saying to your spirit.

Deuteronomy 29:29 *The secret things belong to the Lord our God: but those things which are revealed belong unto us and to our children for ever, that we may do all the words of this law.*

Only the revealed things are our inheritance. Whatever has not been revealed cannot be part of our lives. A renewed mind is needed to correctly interpret the promptings of the Holy Spirit.

5. We need a healthy and renewed mind to receive power over sin

Romans 7:18-25 - *For I know that nothing good dwells in me, that is, in my flesh; for the willing is present in me, but the doing of the good is not. For the good that I want, I do not do, but I practice the very evil that I do not want. But if I am doing the very thing I do not want, I am no longer the one doing it, but sin which dwells in me. I find then the principle that evil is present in me, the one who wants to do good.*

For I joyfully concur with the law of God in the inner man, but I see a different law in the members of my body, waging war against the law of my mind and making me a prisoner of the law of sin which is in my members. Wretched man that I am! Who will set me free from the body of this death? Thanks be to God through Jesus Christ our Lord! So then, on the one hand I myself with my mind am serving the law of God, but on the other, with my flesh the law of sin.

Romans 8:1-2 - *Therefore there is now no condemnation for those who are in Christ Jesus. For the law of the Spirit of life in Christ Jesus has set you free from the law of sin and of* *death.*

We need to realise that we cannot receive power over sin (the wrong disposition that generates thoughts) without a renewed mind.

Why? Because our body is perpetually programmed towards the flesh and our spirit is programmed towards the Spirit of God. The battleground is our mind. So whoever wins that battle will determine what we do.

We cannot convert our body. So when the rapture takes place we will take on glorified bodies, since this body can't get into to heaven. The body was formed in Genesis 2, verse 6 and 7 for the purpose of interacting with earth alone. It is an earth suit. If we are going into space, we take on a space suit.

If we are going to heaven, we take on a heavenly suit. We call this a glorified body. Trying to convert this body is a hopeless task. Forget it. But we can bring this body into subjection through the control of the spirit by the renewal of our minds.

This is because when our mind begins to be renewed it will begin to work in conjunction and in cooperation with our spirit. In this way we can defeat the longings of the flesh.

DEVELOPING INTO MATURITY: *Exercises for developing a healthy and renewed mind.*

DISCIPLINE

Hebrews 5:14 – *But solid food belongs to those who are of full age, that is, those who by reason of use have their senses exercised to discern both good and evil..*

What kind of exercise is the Bible talking about? Well, if I began to go to the gym diligently every day, and put in two or three hours there, in a few months you would not recognise me because I would have become like Mr Universe. What had developed my muscles would have been the exercises. In the same way you have to exercise yourself spiritually. How do you do that as a believer?

Earlier in the book, I said that even if you were an unbeliever, your spirit could still be exercised. That is why you have people who are into divination, for example. You have witches and witchcraft, people who read tarot cards and crystal balls. The reason they can do all that is because they have exercised their human spirits.

The difference is that their spirits are alive to the evil world and our own spirits are alive to God.

Since the devil is a spirit entity as well, they are still communicating with the spirit realm even though they are not saved.

So what are the exercises for developing a healthy mind?

2 Corinthians 10:3-6 - *For though we walk in the flesh, we do not war according to the flesh. For the weapons of our warfare are not carnal but mighty in God for pulling down strongholds, casting down arguments and every high thing that exalts itself against the knowledge of God, bringing every thought into captivity to the obedience of Christ, and being ready to punish all disobedience when your obedience is fulfilled.*

What does that mean? It means that you cannot win your warfare if you do not bring your thoughts captive to the obedience of Christ. It means you cannot win your warfare if your thoughts go out of control all the time. That is the bottom line.

For you to be able to win your spiritual battle, you have to bring your thoughts into the obedience of Christ. You must challenge your thought life so it aligns with that of Christ. As a thought is coming in (when it gets to the gateway of your heart) you ask yourself, *Okay,* now, does this look like what Christ would do? If the answer is no, get rid of that thought immediately.

So all thoughts that come into your heart are thoughts that have been filtered in such a way that they are now in obedience to Christ. It is important that we guard our hearts this way.

Five simple exercises can help us develop a healthy mind. As we bring our thoughts into line with the Word of God, we develop stability in our lives, maturity in our spiritual life and character in our personal life. The three consequences of having a healthy mind are **stability, maturity** and **character.** There is no way you can have those three things without having a healthy mind.

STABILITY
This means being stable in yourself. One of the things I explained in a previous chapter is that you compare yourself with somebody else because you don't have confidence in who you are. But stability is one of the consequences of a healthy mind. You know what God has told you, and so you stand firm on the solid rock.

MATURITY
Somebody once defined maturity as the ability to delay immediate gratification. Maturity

means you know your reward will come but you are not demanding it right now because you understand that God has his perfect time in mind. Maturity brings consistency into your life. It means you can see things the way they ought to be. One of the signs of immaturity is trying hard to justify a wrong decision.

Maturity tends to look at the bigger picture. It stops looking at who is right, and begins to look at what is right. In a marital or any relationship we could reach a point where if we wanted to insist on who was right we could be fighting every day. Because you will have five points that are correct, I will have five points that are correct. You will shoot me another five points, I will shoot you another five points... and so it goes on.

We can all focus on the microscopic specifics, but that won't get us anywhere. In the end this issue is no longer about who is right, but what is the right thing to do.

CHARACTER
The third consequence is character, a generic word that embodies integrity, holiness, righteousness and other things. Character is a way to describe somebody who lives up to God's expectations. If you have character it means, for example, you are a person of your

word.

So we have seen three outcomes, as it were, of a healthy mind. Stability, maturity and character are all developed by process.

What are the five exercises for developing a healthy and renewed mind?

Exercise 1 : THINKING

Romans 8:5 - *For those who are according to the flesh set their minds on the things of the flesh, but those who are according to the Spirit, the things of the Spirit.*

Colossians 3:2 - *Set your mind on the things above, not on the things that are on earth.*

One of the exercises you need to engage in to develop a healthy mind is your model or pattern of thinking. What do you think about? The Bible tells us to set our minds on things that are in heaven, rather than on things on the earth.

So what do we think about when we sit down? Do we think about how to buy a house, or how to buy a TV? I am not saying these things are necessarily wrong, but if that is all that captivates us then we have a problem.

We should sit down and begin to think about working for God, of conquering nations for God, about doing exploits for God. If all we think about are material things — me, me, me, me — our mind will become more and more entrenched in the carnality of this world.

Philippians 4:8 (KJV) - *Finally, brethren, whatsoever things are true, whatsoever things are honest, whatsoever things are just, whatsoever things are pure, whatsoever things are lovely, whatsoever things are of good report; if there be any virtue, and if there be any praise, think on these things.*

The Bible tells us to seek first the kingdom of God and his righteousness all other things will be added unto us.

There are five things to remember about thinking:

1. We cannot choose not to think
Sometimes I look at someone and ask, "What are you thinking?" They'll say, "Nothing." But that is not possible. We cannot choose not to think, any more than we can choose not to breathe. We might stop breathing for thirty seconds, but then we have to gasp for breath. Our mind has to be thinking about something. That is why the Bible tells us to guard our heart

with all diligence for out of it flow the issues of life. That's why what goes into our minds matters a lot. It is not something we can switch on and off.

2. We can choose what we think about

Thoughts are not imposed on us. Even if we are being tortured, we can choose to think about our holiday in paradise because others cannot control what we think. We can be forced to look at things, but nobody can force us to think about anything.

In some parts of India people can train themselves not to feel pain. They can take a metal object and put it through their body. Blood will flow but they will still not feel pain. One of the Yoga sayings is, "Detach your thoughts." That means they think about something different, so they won't feel any pain.

We need our minds to tell us when we are feeling pain. For example, if we are having back pain and we take a pain killer, the pain killer doesn't actually take away the *cause* of the pain. It simply secretes a particular enzyme that tells part of your brain to ignore your back pain. It deadens that part of you for the period the tablet is working.

The real cause of the pain is still there, but you

are not feeling it. So when the painkiller wears off, the problem remains. It has been only temporary relief.

If bone rubs against bone and you take a painkiller, even though the bone is still rubbing and getting worse, you still don't physically feel the pain. You can choose the subject of your thoughts.

3. We cannot think two different thoughts simultaneously.

The way our thinking works is like this: every time we swallow, we have to stop breathing. But we do it so often that we don't notice it. Try it and see. We just cannot breathe and swallow at the same time. Our epiglottis is like a flap. There are two openings in what we call our throat. One goes into our windpipe and one goes into our stomach. Whenever we use one, the flap closes on the other.

That is not a problem for us because we eat all the time and it happens in a moment. In the same way, it is impossible to think two thoughts simultaneously. We cannot think about our spouse and our child at the same time.

Why is it important to realise this? If we can only think of one thought at time, it is easier for us to get rid of specific thoughts we don't want. There is no confusion. If you happen to be thinking a wrong thought at a particular time, you know what that wrong thought is.

4. We are often shocked by our own thoughts. If we are honest with ourselves, after we have thought about something, we may say to ourselves, "You mean I was thinking about *that*?"

Sometime we are shocked at the kinds of things we think about. Some of us have seen ourselves as James Bond, doing all kinds of things. When I drive and see the way some people drive, I tell my wife I wish I had James Bond's car, the one that can fly. It can go into water, and it can puncture somebody else's tyre without that person knowing who did it.

Yes, sometimes our own thoughts surprise us. This is particularly true for children. We are amazed at the kinds of things they think about. When they tell us what they are thinking, we wonder how on earth it got into their heads at that age.

5. Our thoughts can be true and false. They can create realities in our lives but they do not necessarily relate with the realities outside. Recently in Virginia, Washington and Maryland, people were afraid of snipers after some random shooting. People were not buying petrol anymore, and all the supermarkets are empty. On TV I heard that in one particular one month, the sniper killed ten people in three states; but the normal day-to-day gang shooting kills that many people in a week in just *one* of those states. Yet everybody was afraid of the gunman. I am not minimising what this evil man did but my point is that the fear of being shot was greater than the reality.

So the thoughts in our mind can be either true or false. In other words, our thinking about something does not make it real. I used to have a vivid imagination. Because I liked to be prepared for things, I would imagine all the different permutations of what could happen. The Holy Spirit said to me, "What exactly are you doing?" I said I was covering all possibilities. Then he said, "What do you mean by that? Don't you think you are creating these events by your thoughts?" Immediately after that I said to myself, "No more!"

Our realities are being informed by the things we have conceived. Our thoughts can be right, or they can be wrong. We need to grasp this. Our thoughts affect our emotions. They affect our moods and even our physical health. We must crucify the flesh by developing a healthy mind. How do we do this? We do an exercise called Displacement, based on Archimedes Principle.

A body displaces its own weight in the fluid in which it floats. So if we put an object in a bucket of water, the water level rises. How much it rises depends on the volume of the object.

If I want a bubble bath at home I need to keep the water level low. Because if I fill the tub to the brim and then step into the water, I will flood the bathroom. My wife might fill the tub up to halfway, and by time she steps in the water will just about spill over.

The displacement theory also works with our thought patterns. Consider the mind as having a finite amount of space, and we have all sorts of junk stored in it from sleazy TV shows, Mills & Boon, bad music and the like. Whenever we want to make a decision, our mind sees all those things and makes a decision according to the flesh.

The displacement theory, however, ensures that the more of the Word of God we put in our minds, the more the negative thoughts are displaced. This means we don't even need to fully understand the Scriptures.

As we go into the other exercises, we will see

they are all connected. This means that if we decide to confess just ten to twenty scriptures every day, read the Word of God, listen to audio tapes and just get the Word into our spirit, it will force those negative thoughts out of our mind.

That is how our thought patterns work. We have to begin to eat the Word of God, as it were. Somebody called me the other day to tell me she was going through some hard times and it was difficult for her to pray or to study God's Word. I told her she had to be creative in the way she studied it.

If something was true, I told her, she might not feel like opening the Bible to study it. But I have certain Christian videos at home which I slot in. By the time I have finished watching one, I've jotted down two pages of study notes. This is another way of hearing the Word but without a studious approach.

So we need to be exploring other ways of hearing the Word of God. It can be through different media —not just when we open the Bible.

Often when a negative thought approaches me, I reject it in the name of Jesus. I banish it to the pits of hell and refuse to let it in. Whenever we do that, you find the thought disappears. This is an exercise we you have to engage in. Success is not an accident. Nor does a healthy mind just creep up on us. It is something you have to make an effort to develop. You see a boy in class, you look at him and think, hmm, he's not bad. You begin to think you would like to sit close to him. You thoughts begin to inform your action.

Before you know it, things begin to happen as a result of that one thought which you should have rejected. Remember, no one— not even the devil — can impose a thought on you. You have the right to decide and to choose what you think about.

So stop making excuses. "I just couldn't control it" is a lie. The displacement theory says we can control our thoughts and as we constantly bring into our minds the Word of God, the things of God and the thoughts of God, they displace the negative thoughts. It happens automatically. Even if you don't understand the scripture yet, just keep saying it. It may not go into your conscious mind but it will at least go into your subconscious mind. Either way, you are pushing out the negative thought.

Exercise 2: THE POWER OF IMAGINATION

To imagine something is to deliberately picture what we have been thinking and participate mentally in it.

This means that if we don't arrest a negative pattern of thinking it deteriorates into wrong imagination. We must educate our minds to see what we hear so they do not reject the dimension of the spirit.

When the Bible says faith comes by hearing and hearing by the Word of God, it means faith comes by hearing and *understanding* the Word of God. We must educate our mind to begin to picture what we hear.

There are two gateways to our imagination: our eyes and our ears, and we need to guard them when it comes to our imagination. What we see determines the picture we get and what we hear determines the sound we hear. Under the right circumstances imagination becomes a higher form of thinking.

Sometimes when our imagination is at work, we begin to talk to ourselves based on a particular situation we are imagining. When we begin to mentally participate with our thoughts, it becomes imagination; it is no longer thought.

By exercising imagination we increase the borders of our mind and break free from our mental limitations.

If you can arrest the pattern of our thinking, it is easy for us to deal with our wrong imagination. That is why I said these things work together. If your thoughts are already filtered, the kind of mental picture you can have becomes a filtered one. This is how to have a renewed mind.

A good example is when we are praying in the spirit. The Bible says when we pray in the spirit our understanding in unfruitful. One of the things I have noticed is that it is possible to be praying in the spirit (that is, speaking in tongues) and engaging in unrelated and trivial thoughts like cooking dinner at the same time.

This leads to lip service rather than productive prayer, because we need to participate mentally in what we are praying about. If we are praying for the growth of the church, for example, as we pray we begin to visualise the hall being filled with people.

We begin to see two services taking place. We are participating mentally with the object of our prayer. When we do this it is easy for God to drop an answer in your heart.

But when we are already cooking rice in our mind when we are supposed to be praying for the growth of the church, we are on a different frequency from God, and we know that two radios on different frequencies cannot communicate.

By exercise, our minds get accustomed to such expansions and soon allow faith to flourish. We need to wilfully create pictures in agreement with the Rhema Word. This is particularly important in worship and prophecy.

We need to filter our thoughts based on the word of God. Then it is easy for us to have a healthy imagination because imagination is a higher form of thinking. When we mentally participate with the object of your thought, we are no longer thinking about it—we are imagining it.

The root is the thought, and once we arrest the thought we can easily arrest what we imagine. We need to arrest our thoughts, bringing them to the obedience of Christ, and once we do that we can begin to develop the mind of Christ. We cannot develop a healthy mind if we keep imagining the wrong things.

We cannot develop a healthy mind if we imagine ourselves stealing, fornicating, lying, committing robbery, etc. We can begin to see ourselves doing the right things but only after we have filtered the thoughts that arrive in the first place. So one builds on the other.

Exercise 3: MEMORISATION
We have three basic mental capacities:
- To remember and retain
- To receive new information and facts and assimilate them

  For example, if I asked you for your birth date you would tell me, not because you knew it all along but because somebody told you. If you parents celebrated the wrong birthday for you, you would have the wrong information.

  My father-in-law celebrated his birthday in February for more than 50 years. Then he saw a document saying he was born in April. So we know our birth date because we have been told it, and retain that information. We can receive new information and assimilate it. That is why it is good to understand that learning is life-long. We are always learning.
- To reason and come to a logical conclusion.

One of the key ways of developing a healthy mind is to memorise scriptures and the ways and things of God. Sadly, many Christians today are mentally lazy. They have want their pastors to pray for them, read the Bible for them, chase the devil away for them, win their battles for them and all they have to do is pay for the privilege. People like this go carry holy water and holy oil all over the place and they can't even substantiate their position with a single scripture.

The patience of memorisation, the ability to memorise scriptures and spiritual information is a necessary part of developing a healthy mind. In John 14:26 the Bible says the Holy Spirit brings into our remembrance the things we have learned. To memorise is to wilfully retain facts and information revealed to us by the Holy Spirit and to commit them to memory.

The discipline or ability to memorise and retain what the Holy Spirit has said is essential to our spiritual growth. We have the capacity both to retain and to recall information. Even if we have difficulty in remembering, the Bible says the Holy Spirit's job is to help us to remember those facts and that information.

The Holy Spirit cannot remind you of what you have not first learnt. I tell young Christians that when it comes to learning scriptures, not to worry if they cannot remembering the things immediately. They must just do their bit and study the scriptures. When we come to specific situations in life when you need them, the Holy Spirit will remind us about them. He will bring them to our remembrance.

But the Holy Spirit cannot multiply something out of nothing. He needs a seed. We must have at least gotten that information in the first place. There are times when God in his sovereignty reveals to us scriptural facts that we have not learnt before. But that does not happen every day. In the end, it is still the truth you know that will set you free.

Our job is to study the scriptures; the Holy Spirit's job is to remind us of them. If we don't plant a seed, there is nothing for God to multiply.

"Pastor, I read the Bible in the morning, and by evening, I have almost forgotten everything I have read." Fine, just keep reading it. We are to ponder and think and continue to assess the words of the Spirit.

The Holy Spirit can only bring to remembrance what we have heard, read and committed to memory. We do the memorisation, the Holy Spirit does the reminding. Memorisation is one of the key exercises for developing a healthy mind. Why?

Because when a negative thought comes, immediately the Holy Spirit brings to our remembrance a scripture that relates to it: don't think about this, don't do that. So through the patience and practice of memorisation, we can recall God's word and use it to develop a healthy mind and extinguish negative thoughts as and when necessary.

The children of Israel were told to remember many things. In Numbers 15:39, Deuteronomy 8:2, Joshua 1:13, and many other scriptures, God keeps saying, remember, remember.

In Proverbs 3:1, the Bible says, *my son do not forget my teaching but let your heart keep my commandment.* We need to train our memory to retain information.

How do we train our minds to memorise?

1. Write down all inspired thoughts. There are many times where maybe a prophecy is said over our life or suddenly the Holy Spirit reveals certain thoughts to our spirit. We write this down so we don't forget it.

2. Voice all inspired thoughts. When we talk about, sing about or pray about what the Holy Spirit has spoken into our hearts, our faith is consolidated. Many of us underestimate the power of confession because it has been abused, and so many think it is not important.

But it is absolutely vital. Saying with your own mouth what God has said about you is crucial to developing your faith.

The Bible says in Philemon that the communication of our faith may become effectual by our acknowledgement of every good thing that is in us in Christ Jesus. Hearing yourself saying you can make it, strengthens your resolve.

I tell myself every day, "Because I have a covenant of distinction with God, I will not partake of the frustrations of this generation." I don't care what the enemy throws at me. The fact that the enemy is throwing something at us shows we are doing something right.

One of my mentors once said, *if you are going on a journey and you have not met the devil, you must be going in the same direction as he.* Champions are birthed in the furnace of affliction. The Bible says God will not allow us to be tested beyond what we can bear, and even when we are being tested he provides a way of escape.

Who decides what we can bear? It is God, not us, because if we decide what we can bear, we only need to do something tiny before we say, "Look God! See how far I am jumping!" We need to understand that every time God allows us to go through things it is because he wants to bring out something inside us that we have not realised. He wants to re-ignite a passion or a gift he has given us which we are not using. He wants to re-ignite a talent that we have allowed to stay dormant for too long.

If God will not allow us to be tempted beyond what we can bear, it means that what we are going through right now is known by God. We are going through it because he knows we can bear it.

We cannot mature in God without going through these things. To become an exceptional person in God, we need to go through exceptional situations. If we want to be extraordinary we have to have conquered extraordinary enemies. We cannot be extraordinary by going through ordinary things that everybody else is going through.

Those whom God will raise to greater heights in him are those who will go through exceptional difficulties —difficulties that will seem peculiar to them. The size of your challenge is an indication of God's estimation of you.

The more God thinks of you the bigger will be your struggle. But as we have said, he knows you can bear it. Remember the book of Job? After Job began to complain, he accused God of losing control, of not caring.

God was furious with him, and from chapter 38 onwards the Lord fired 70 questions at Job. Who are you to accuse me of losing control? Where were you when I created the universe? Do you know how the birds in the sky stay up there? At the end Job repented of his thoughts towards God, even though his questions were still not answered.

Job came to realise that God was in control, and that since his life was in God's hands he had nothing to worry about. With Job we may say, *I may not fully know where you are taking me with this situation, Lord, but I know you know what you are doing.*

If I tell my children, we are going to Scotland tomorrow for example, they won't know where Scotland is, or how long the journey will take. I may decide to go to Southampton first, but that is not their problem. They just know that if they get into the car, Daddy will eventually get them to Scotland.

That is how to relate to God. Jesus once said to his disciples, "Let us go over to the other side." Halfway across they run into a storm and they ask him, "Don't you care that we perish?" Jesus says, "Hold on a second! Where did I tell you we were going? The other side. Does this look like the other side to you? No!"

So regardless of the storms that come our way, if Jesus tells us he is taking us to the other side, we will get there. Storms will come, but we need to understand that our destination has been pronounced by God and the devil cannot short-circuit our victory.

Don't allow your mind to become your enemy. The worst thing God can do to any of us is to leave us to our own devices. We'll self-destruct in five seconds, without the enemy's help! The Bible says there is a way that seems right to a man, but the end of it is destruction. God is trying to save us from ourselves, not from the enemy. The devil is an easy battle!

So write down all your inspired thoughts, and voice all your inspired thoughts.

3. Retain portions of Scripture in your mind that link with the thoughts.
Try to remember whole passages. If you can't remember them verbatim, try to remember the essence of each one. If you're a Bible student, you'll know each book of the Bible and each chapter of each book has a theme running

through it. Sometimes you can tell somebody what God is saying and the person can tell you which book it is from. They might even tell you what chapter it's from, although they might not remember the verse. Once we remember the essence of a book, we've already obtained half of its message. That's why we need memorisation.

A healthy mind does not come to us by accident. We need to develop it deliberately.

Exercise 4: VISUALISATION
Visualisation is the process of allowing the Holy Spirit to activate our spirit, to communicate to it a message from God, and to release that information to our minds.

Visualisation is somewhat linked to, and sometimes confused, with imagination. The difference between them is that visualisation is like a video and imagination is like a still picture. Visualisation is more dynamic, and sometimes expresses itself in visions and dreams. When God gives us a picture of what is happening in a situation, we have a vision or a dream of the event.

That process goes beyond the use of our imagination. We are now interacting with the realities of what is going on. The Holy Spirit gives our human spirit particular information and through visualisation we are able to move that information forward. We yield our mind and our spirit to the activity of the Holy Spirit and allow him to speak to us in various ways, including visions and dreams. (Joel chapter 2 explains this).

A few years ago, God showed me a vision about how the United Kingdom would be revived. I shared this with one of my close friends and he told me it agreed with the vision God has also shared with him. In the vision God gave me, I seemed to be in the sky, looking down over the UK. On one side of the country I saw a huge fire that had started burning while the rest of the land was cold. As that fire started to spread towards the other side, it began to lose some of its brightness. After a while it died, because everything it was coming into contact with on the way was extinguishing it.

Then it was as though the Lord took me to a different area and again I looked over the whole of the land. But in this second vision I saw small fires in different nooks and crannies, like little torches of fire.

God said to me, "Watch!" As those little fires burned and the wind began to blow, one fire began to touch one next to it until there were thousands of little fires. And so the inferno grew. The wind would blow again, and before I knew it, the whole city was ablaze. God told me this was how revival would take place in this city and nation.

"How do you mean?" I asked. God answered, "It will take place by the torch of righteousness. The fire of revival will begin to burn on every street corner, not just in one massive church or massive organisation". It has not happened in America, where they have churches of forty to fifty thousand. And why have some of the so-called revivals in other parts of the world not been effective? That is obvious.

They have been localised. A revival is supposed to ignite in one place and then spread across the land where it will have a wide impact. When the spirit of the Lord begins to move in revival, he does not stop at the county border.

I've used this vision as an example of how God can use pictures to communicate with you. Sometimes we have watched horror films before sleeping and then have dreamed of butterflies biting us in the backside.

But that's not what I mean by dreams here. Nor do I mean, when I speak of vision, a particular direction that God is giving us. Vision here is like a trance. We might be sitting down studying the Word, when suddenly we seem to be taken out of that environment and find ourselves in an imaginary world that we can interact with. God is using that to communicate a particular message to us.

We have arranged these exercises in a deliberate order. We cannot begin to use visualisation as a way of developing our minds if we haven't been able to grasp the first three exercises. Each builds on the last. If you are still having a problem with thought patterns haven't been arrested, you won't arrive at the place where visualisation can work in your life.

God needs to be able to trust that your mind will be able to interpret what he is telling your spirit. You cannot walk in the gifts of the Spirit, such as the word of knowledge, the word of prophecy and the rest, if you do not have a renewed mind. This is the core of Christianity. Christianity is not the sinner's prayer, or even a positive confession of faith. Christianity is our ability to win the mind battle. It is our ability to renew our mind that determines whether or not we can reflect Christ.

The renewal of our mind does not happen by accident. It is an ongoing effort. That is why the Bible speaks of a *renewing*. It is a continuous thing, day by day, until Jesus comes.

We can, however, get our mind to a state whereby it works in co-operation with our spirit. That is what these exercises are about. The process of visualisation is a bit more advanced than the others we have been dealing with, but one progresses to the next.

Exercise 5: THE JOY OF MEDITATION

Christian meditation is the process of thinking on, imagining, memorising and progressively developing the Rhema word or revelation we have received.

Meditation involves thinking on God's spoken word until first, we understand its meaning, secondly, we know its implications, and thirdly, we know the degree of our involvement and participation in that word. In a fourth stage we develop a balanced, wholesome truth around God's revealed word to us.

How does meditation work?
First, it involves our receiving a word from God. This may be a Rhema for ourselves or a revelation of God's written word for a corporate purpose.

Secondly, after we receive that word we begin to think along the lines of this revealed word.

Thirdly, we start to interpret what we have just received from God. That means considering the revealed facts in the light of what we already know. We search our subconscious mind for keys, clues and experiences to help us to interpret it. Usually when we are meditating, we tend to need to come to an inspired conclusion at the end of it.

Let us say, for example, that we are asking God how to revive this city. We begin to study the Word of God, and suddenly a scripture jumps out to us which seems to tell us what strategy we should employ. That is a product of meditation.

So what is God telling us to do now? We map out the details of our action plan, to carry out the conclusion we have reached. In meditation we not only know that God has spoken; we also know *what* he has spoken. So we know the type of response that is required of us. In meditation we receive the required strategies for taking over say the land.

And in our nations we particularly need strategies. The Bible says the heart of a king is in the hands of the Lord. God knows how the nations of the world can be reached. Many years ago a missionary went to a village in South America (which we will call Village A) here all the people were idol worshippers. As part of his efforts to get them saved he told them how God had sent his Son to die. But this angered them.

"How can you tell us God sent his Son to die?" they demanded. "It doesn't make sense!"

For nine years this missionary toiled in that village, with just two in his congregation. The chief told the villagers not to listen to him, but the missionary refused to leave. In the ninth year, there was a war between Village A and its more powerful neighbour (which we'll call village B).

In the first battle hundreds of people died. So the chief of Village A sent a message to the chief of Village B.

"Look," he said, "if we continue this battle, you will kill all of us, or most of us, and many of your own people will die too. It doesn't make sense. Let's come together."

So the two chiefs met, and agreed they would not attack each other again. Then the chief of Village A, which was militarily weaker, said, "How will I know you will keep your word?"

"Here's what I will do," said Chief B. "Your first

daughter is single, isn't she? Okay, my first son is single too. I will give my son to marry your daughter, as a sign of the unity of the two villages. As long as the two remain married, it will not be in our interest to attack each other's villages."

And that is what happened. Later this missionary was praying and God told him this was the key to getting through to the people. So he started saying to them, "Remember my telling you how God sent his Son as a mediator between man and God? And how you told me it was not possible? Now look at what Chief B has done!"

He explained how the giving in marriage of chief B's son to Chief A's daughter had been a way mediating between the two villages. In the tenth year, 80 percent of the village got saved, because the missionary's story had suddenly become credible. Through one practical example they now understood how somebody could be a mediator.

The point I am making is this: for nine years this guy could have given up, but he knew there had to be a key to unlocking the hearts of the people. Every previous strategy had not worked. But God told him this peace-making event was the key he needed.

There must be a key to reach the people of this nation and every other nation. We don't know it yet, which is why we need meditation to discover this key which will unlock the nations to the gospel of grace.

Summary
To develop a healthy mind, we need the five exercises of thinking, imagination, memorisation, visualisation and meditation.

There are three sources of influence on the mind of a person. We have the Holy Spirit via the human spirit, we have the human spirit in itself, and we have the external gateways of eyes and ears. Through these mind-renewing exercises we can become effective in our walk with God.

Wrong thoughts lead to wrong emotions, and wrong emotions lead to wrong living. We cannot live right if we think wrongly. Who we are reflects the way we think. If we always think of ourselves as a victim, we will be a victim. Our thinking creates our realities.

I pray this book will challenge you to get to know God more and to take advantage of the massive resources God has given you. We need to renew our minds so we can display the excellence of Christ in all circumstances.

1 John 3:2 (NIV) - *Dear friends, now we are children of God, and what we will be has not yet been made known. But we know that when Christ appears we shall be like him, for we shall see him as he is.*

2 Corinthians 3:18 (NIV) - *And we all, who with unveiled faces contemplate[a] the Lord's glory, are being transformed into his image with ever-increasing glory, which comes from the Lord, who is the Spirit.*

You are child of the King, it is time to go out and win. It is a new day. God bless you.

Note here your Key Learning Points from Chapter 3

PART B

NOW LET THE BATTLE BEGIN

Now that you know how to become a prepared vessel and weapon in the hands of God (through the renewal of your mind); you are ready for the battle to reclaim the marketplace for God. From now on every instruction will make more sense to you, for you are battle ready. So let the battle strategy commence....

CHAPTER 4

OUR CALLING TO THE MARKETPLACE

Knowing we have been called into the marketplace; in this book I want to show you your part and more importantly how you can access the marketplace successfully as a follower of Jesus.

You need to understand the predominant intention of God, because if you're not advancing that intention you might be trying to do the right thing for the wrong reason and end up not succeeding.

It's as you were a manager employed by a premiership club. You have been told clearly that the intention of the owner of club is to win the champions' league. The owner doesn't care where the team is on the premiership table. He is only interested in the champions' league. So you, as the manager, need to understand that you can play all the good football you like, and you can even top the premiership league, but if you don't make that Champions' League — let alone win it — you have failed as far as the owner is concerned. This is because you have not advanced the purpose for which the owner employed you.

So engagement in the marketplace is not about starting a business, even though that might be involved. It's about starting a business *for the right reason.* We are going to look at the strategic invasion of the marketplace in this book, from both biblical and practical perspectives.

Paradigm Shifts Needed
There are certain paradigm shifts that need to take place in our lives if we are going to understand what God is doing in these last days to reclaim the marketplace. We need to tune in to heaven's frequency, see what God sees, and think the way he thinks if we are to be effective agents and tools in his hand for wealth transfer. Here are some of the new paradigms we will need.

1. We are called to disciple nations and not just individuals
When we hear the word "discipleship" in church,

it tends to relate to individuals or small groups. "I'm going to discipleship class" is a common statement. We are used to individual discipleship. This is not wrong, but it is essentially incomplete. God actually instructs us to make *disciples of nations*.

Nations are important to God, for territories must be taken if his kingdom is to be extended. In the Old Testament most of the words spoken by the prophets were directed at nations and only a few addressed individuals. We need to take territories and disciple nations.

Therefore, go and make disciples of all the nations, baptizing them in the name of the Father and of the Son and of the Holy Spirit." — *Matthew 28:19*

Of course, individuals are essential to what God is going to do, but our objective is to be kingdom ambassadors. As noted in Matthew 28, we are to focus on nations, not just individuals. That is God's agenda. To start thinking globally is the kingdom mandate.

2. We need to understand that the marketplace, which is the heart of the nation, has been redeemed and now needs to be reclaimed for God.
This concept will become clearer as we go

along. But one thing to note is that every time the word "marketplace" has been used in the church, many have tended to link it to business and the economy.

This is an incomplete understanding. The "marketplace" describes what makes a nation. So all aspects of nationhood constitute the marketplace. As we go on, you will see how many of these aspects there. So the marketplace is not about the business or economic sectors alone.

What is the point of focusing on business alone when the people who make the rules affecting businesses are ungodly? If we say we are a believer and strictly into business, the ungodly person who controls politics could easily make a law tomorrow and put us *out* of business. So the marketplace is about every aspect of the nation that we are supposed to invade with righteousness.

3. Every Christian is a minister and all our work is spiritual, whether we are in or out of "church" as we know it.
Part of the reason we are short of labourers in the church is that many have developed the mentality that the pastor is "the minister" and the rest of us mere followers. As a result you have a church of 1,000 with twenty pastors who are

doing most of the work while the remaining 980 are spectators. That's not what it should be!

"Now all things are of God, who has reconciled us to himself through Jesus Christ, and has given us the ministry of reconciliation". 2 Corinthians 5:18

What we do might be different with each person, but everybody has a ministry. Also, if we are invading the marketplace with righteousness, everything we do is spiritual in nature, whether we work for Barclays Bank or Microsoft. This because we are supposed to have presence everywhere. We will explore this more later.

4. We are called to take the kingdom of God to where the kingdom of darkness is entrenched, for Jesus to build his church.
In other words, we are not called to stay within the four walls of a building called church. We are not supposed to be running from darkness as some Christians do, in an effort to remain in the comfort zone. The whole idea is for us to impact darkness, not to be running from it.

5. Transformation of the city and nation will not take place until believers stop being idle in the market place.
That is the fundamental challenge for our generation. Transformation cannot happen if

believers continue to be idle in the market place. I say "idle" because all of us are already in the market place in one way or another.

In fact, we spend most of our days, weeks, and months there. We are active in "church" but idle in the marketplace and the devil loves it! He doesn't mind our having a million-member church as long as we stay busy inside the building but lazy where it really matters.

And he went out about the third hour and saw others standing idle in the marketplace...- Matthew 20:3

We have been idle there long enough. It is time for action. So these fundamental paradigms will need to be embraced by us if we are to succeed in the marketplace and better understand the principles revealed in this book.

Matthew 28:18-20 – *Jesus came to them and said, "All authority has been given to me in heaven and on earth. Go therefore and disciple all the nations, baptizing them in the name of the Father and of the Son and of the Holy Spirit, and teaching them to obey all that I have commanded you. And surely I am with you always, to the very end of the age."*

That's the last thing the Lord said in the book of

Matthew. The scripture tells us to go and disciple all the *nations*, but after the word "nation," everything appears to apply to *individuals*. Is there a contradiction here? How do we teach and baptize nations in the name of the Father, Son and Holy Ghost? How do we teach nations to observe all that God commands?

Revelation is needed to fully understand the things of the Spirit. In Matthew 28:18-20 God is not ignoring people. He is simply saying that *our outreach to people must be within a framework of national transformation.* Christians usually reach people in order to fill churches. But God is saying emphatically that the purpose of reaching people is so that *nations can be transformed.*

True evangelism and outreach is not practised simply to increase church membership numbers. Our evangelism must be to impact territories so that like Titus — one man who impacted all of Crete — our presence in a community or nation transforms that nation for Christ. It's not about church increase; it's about kingdom increase.

Any teaching, any baptizing we're doing for individuals that is not within the *framework of national transformation* is not God's objective.

As a result many of our churches are full but there is unrighteousness all around us and our communities are being less and less impacted by the gospel.

There are nations where you find a church on every corner, yet unrighteousness, corruption and sin are ruling the land. Are we about increasing the size of the church numerically or taking territories and nations for God?

Sadly, many Christian leaders like to boast of their mega churches. But the vital questions for them are: How have you affected your nation? How have you affected your city? How have you impacted your society?

The Word says, "Go therefore and disciple all the nations." That's what we're here to do. By the grace of God, as we you read on, we will begin to see our part in this kingdom commission.

In Acts 1:8 we read: *"But you shall receive power when the Holy Spirit has come upon you; and you shall be witnesses to me...."*

Does the Bible say, "...in your churches"? No.

Acts 1:8 continues; *"...you shall be witnesses to me in Jerusalem, and in all Judea and Samaria, and to the end of the earth."*

You can see that the Bible's response is still about cities and nations and taking territories. We need to change our paradigm from the local church to the Kingdom, The Bible says further on:

"...Did we not strictly command you not to teach in this name? And look, you have filled Jerusalem with your teaching..." **Acts 5:28**

What the city captains and officials were complaining about was that rather than just fraternising in their little buildings called church, the disciples had filled the entire city with their teachings and values. They had transformed it by transforming the people.

Disciple of cities and nations should be the focus of the church today. It is not about some mega church prospering in the midst of a poverty-stricken community.

Filling Jerusalem with our teaching is not about going to preach at work or in the marketplace. It is about our lives being so transformed that we become transformative in everything we do. It is about allowing our lifestyle to speak righteousness and excellence.

It is about allowing our Bible-inspired values to

dictate our performance, attitudes and responses at work and in business.

Key principles: We need to raise our ambitions and our faith expressions. We cannot disciple nations without engaging with the *instruments and institutions* of the nation state. What are they? These instruments and institutions have a metaphorical name in the Bible. They are referred to as *mountains.* But I also use the word *sector* instead of *mountain* from time to time.

In Isaiah 2:2-3 we read:
"Now it shall come to pass in the latter days that the mountain of the Lord's house shall be established on the top of the mountains, and shall be exalted above the hills; and all nations shall flow to it. Many people shall come and say, "Come, and let us go up to the mountain of the Lord, to the house of the God of Jacob. He will teach us his ways, and we shall walk in his paths." For out of Zion shall go forth the law, and the word of the Lord from Jerusalem.

In other words, there are certain mountains (institutions or sectors) in every nation. But the Bible says the mountain *of the Lord's house* will be exalted above all others.

We are to begin a strategic invasion of the marketplace. The purpose of this invasion (which began when Christ came to earth) is to take over every domain on earth.

God desires to indwell his people, so he can position them in strategic places for the advancement of his kingdom and for the benefit of his people who are connected to him in every sphere of life (Jeremiah 3:14-23). Just as the Ark of the Covenant represented the presence of God, the people whom God brings to Mount Zion are those who carry his presence.

In other words, God wants to bring us to Mount Zion where he will indwell and fill us so that we can bring transformation, by his power, to every field of human endeavor. This is for the extension of his kingdom and the betterment of his people.

His foundation is in the holy mountains. The Lords loves the gates of Zion more than all the dwellings of Jacob. Glorious things are spoken of you, O city of God...' –**Psalm 87: 1-6**.

Truly in vain is salvation hoped for from the hills, and from the multitude of mountains: truly in the LORD our God is the salvation of Israel." – **Jeremiah 3:23**

So we know that mountains exist in nations. They are metaphors for the institutions of the nation state and societal culture. But the enemies of God presently occupy them, and so God is raising up a people who will invade the camp of the enemy and take back these mountains.

The church has ignored them for too long. We have been busy looking inwards, meeting with ourselves, celebrating with ourselves and enjoying each other's company. We've become so focused on church activities that we've missed our call to transform our society and nation. Of what use is the salt that stays in the saltshaker?

Going Beyond the Red Sea
The Bible says the mountain of the Lord's house will be exalted *above all the mountains*. These are societal and cultural mountains. The Lord will raise up his own people and through them he will occupy these mountains in the nations. What are these mountains that make up nations?

In dealing with the strategic invasion of the marketplace, we need to understand that the nations God has given to us to dominate are the equivalent of our Promised Land.
God said, "Ask of me and I will give you the

nations" (Psalm 2:8). If Egypt represents where we were in our sin, the Promised Land is the nation God is calling us to. The crossing of the Red Sea symbolizes our being born again (red suggests blood), so in being saved we are escaping from Egypt.

But there is one more crossing we need to make before we enter our Promised Land. We must cross the River Jordan. (We will be looking at this principle in more detail later.) For so long in the church we've crossed the Red Sea and then sat down! But that doesn't get us into the Promised Land.

Many of us have been camped beside the River Jordan all our lives, waiting but seeing nothing happening. In fact many of us are so used to the wilderness that we now want God to bless us right there. But God is saying, "I am not going to do that. The wilderness is not my plan or destination for you."

The Seven Enemies
"When the Lord your God brings you into the land which you go to possess, and has cast out many nations before you, the Hittites and the Girgashites and the Amorites and the Canaanites and the Perizzites and the Hivites and the Jebusites, seven nations greater and mightier than you..." **Deut.7:1 (NKJV)**

The Lord promises to drive out seven nations greater and mightier than us, his people. These seven nations must be conquered before we can possess our own Promised Land. So how do we overcome the Hittites, the Girgashites, and so on? There are many hidden gems in Scripture reserved for those eyes that the Holy Spirit opens to the truth of God's word.

Each of these seven enemies to be confronted equates to one of the seven sectors that make up a nation. If we are to disciple nations, we have to rise to the top of each sector and raise the banner of righteousness on it.

Who, then, are the Hittites? What spirit rules over them? What is the corresponding marketplace sector that we, the people of God, need to take over?

And Joshua said, "By this you shall know that the living God is among you, and that he will without fail drive out from before you the Canaanites and the Hittites and the Hites and the Perizzites and the Girgashites and the Amorites and the Jebusites.- **Joshua 3:10**

These are the same seven nations that were named in Deuteronomy, but in a slightly different order.

So before we possess our Promised Land we must know how to conquer these seven nations. Before the kingdoms of this world can become the kingdoms of our God, according to the book of Revelation, we need to have conquered these seven nations (sectors or mountains). Sadly, the church has largely ignored most of these sectors, to our detriment.

What are the seven sectors of the marketplace?
1. Media
2. Business and Economy
3. Government and Politics
4. Education
5. Arts and Entertainment
6. Family
7. Religion

Every nation has these seven sectors. Once we identify them, we cover the whole nation. The church may think of the marketplace as just the seat of business, but as we have seen already, it's much more than that.

I'll be revealing in this book how each of these nations —the Hittites, Perizzites, Girgashites and so on — equates to one of the seven marketplace sectors and reflects the predominant satanic spirit that controls it.

We know from Scripture that God does not use an untested vessel. He uses those whom he has taken through a process so they can represent him effectively in whatever position he places them. Joseph is a prototype of one whom God took through a process. God then positioned him in a strategic position for the advancement of his kingdom and the benefit of his people.

When God sent Joseph to Egypt ahead of his brothers, he conquered two mountains in Egypt before his brothers arrived. He conquered the mountain of politics and the mountain of economy, to sustain and provide for his entire family. God will place a person in every situation to situate the people where they should be, just as Joseph situated his people in the best part of the land in Egypt.

God is waiting for a generation who will connect to him, so they can properly redistribute the resources of the land (**Genesis 49:22-24**). In this book you will see how the church has abandoned many of these areas to the enemy. Hence Satan has now entrenched himself in all those mountains, at our expense.

In Revelation 5:1 we read: *And I saw in the right hand of him who sat on the throne a scroll written inside and on the back, sealed with seven seals...*

[How many seals? How many mountains to conquer?]

Then I saw a strong angel proclaiming with a loud voice, "Who is worthy to open the scroll and to loose its seals?" [3] And no one in heaven or on the earth under the earth was able to open the scroll, or to look at it.[4]

*So I wept much, because no one was found worthy to open and read the scroll, or to look at it. [5] But one of the elders said to me, "Do not weep. Behold, the Lion of the tribe of Judah, the Root of David, has prevailed to open the scroll and to loose its **seven seals**."*

[6] And I looked, and behold, in the midst of the throne and of the four living creatures, and in the midst of the elders, stood a Lamb as though it had been slain, having seven horns and seven eyes, which are the seven Spirits of God sent out into all the earth.[7] Then he came and took the scroll out of the right hand of him who sat on the throne.

–Rev 5:1-7

How many cities? Seven. How many seals? Seven. I'll explain why later. Read on:

Then I looked, and I heard the voice of many angels around the throne, the living creatures, and the elders; and the number of them was ten thousand times ten thousand, and thousands of

*thousands, **12** saying with a loud voice: "Worthy is the Lamb who was slain to receive **power** and **riches** and **wisdom**, and **strength** and **honour** and **glory** and **blessing**!"*
***13** And every creature which is in heaven and on the earth and under the earth and such as are in the sea, and all that are in them, I heard saying: "Blessing and honour and glory and power Be to Him who sits on the throne, And to the Lamb, forever and ever!"*
– Rev 5:11-13.

Power, riches, wisdom, strength, honour, glory and blessing. Each of these seven things that the Lamb is worthy to receive equates to one of the seven sectors (mountains) and seven nations we have been looking at.

The Lamb is waiting to receive the nations for himself while we have been sitting down thinking it's all about having church services and conferences among ourselves. Because we have failed to impact the nations, we have not advanced God's agenda as we should have.

In Revelation 5, the seven attributes of majesty that the Lamb is worthy to receive coincide with the seven pillars (sectors) of every nation that make up the marketplace. So God is worthy to receive:

Power   which speaks of **Government**
Riches   which speaks of **Economy**
Wisdom   which speaks of **Education**
Strength   which speaks of **Family**
Honour   which speaks of **Religion**
Glory   which speaks of celebration, that is **Arts and Entertainment.**
Blessing   which speaks of **Media**.

All of these will become clearer as we progress. Let us read further in Revelations:

Then one of the seven angels who had the seven bowls came and talked with me, saying to me, "Come I will show you the judgment of the great harlot who sits on many waters, ² with whom the kings of the eth committed fornication, and the inhabitants of the earth were made drunk with the wine of her fornication."
³ So he carried me away in the Spirit into the ilderness. And I saw a woman sitting on a scarlet beast which was full of names of blasphemy, having seven heads and ten horns. ⁴ The woman was arrayed in purple and scarlet, and adorned with gold and precious stones and pearls, having in her hand a golden cup full of abominations and the filthiness of her fornication. ⁵ And on her forehead a name was written: Mystery, Babylon the great, the mother of harlots and of the abominations of the earth.

⁶ I saw the woman, drunk with the blood of the saints and with the blood of the martyrs of Jesus. And when I saw her, I marvelled with great amazement.
⁷ But the angel said to me, "Why did you marvel? will tell you the mystery of the woman and of the beast that carries her, which has the seven heads and the ten horns.⁸ The beast that you saw was, and is not, and will ascend out of the bottomless pit and go to perdition. And those who dwell on the earth will marvel, whose names are not written in the Book of Life from the foundation of the world, when they see the beast that was, and is not, and yet is.
⁹ "Here is the mind which has wisdom: The seven heads are seven mountains on which the woman sits. ¹⁰ There are also seven kings. Five have fallen, one is, and the other has not yet come. And when he comes, he must continue a short time. - **Rev. 17:1-10**

This demonic entity described as a woman or whore must be displaced from the mountains or seats of power, for it is currently holding the nations bound.

Now you see why the Bible says the weapons of our warfare are not carnal, but *mighty* through God. There are demonic forces in operation and the earlier we understand this, the better. Every area we work in or operate in the marketplace is being controlled by the King of Tyre (Satan) and his territorial demons.

So we cannot win without a proper strategy, which we'll be looking at in the following chapters. This is our mission as children of God.

Note here your Key Learning Points from Chapter 4

CHAPTER 5

OVERVIEW OF THE SPIRITUALITY OF THE MARKETPLACE

The earth is the Lord's and the fullness thereof. All the governments and peoples, the earth and all its wealth, belong to our God whose wealth shall yet fill the earth. How is this going to happen? By believers reclaiming the marketplace. The word is *reclaim*.

Adam and Eve once owned it all. So we are simply reclaiming by righteousness what Satan stole through deceit. The marketplace is like the hill of God that has become the garrison of the Philistines in 1 Samuel 10. We need to reclaim it before we can arrive at the Promised Land of *wealth transfer*.

After that you shall come to the hill of God where the Philistine garrison is. And it will happen, when you have come there to the city, that you will meet a group of prophets.... - 1 Samuel 10:5

How did the hill of God become the garrison of the enemy? Because God's people abandoned the hills. So the enemy took over and now rules. Our task in this generation is to dislodge the enemy and reclaim the hills for God.

Seven sectors of all nation states

Seven is a perfect number in Scripture. It represents completion. Seven is mentioned 387 times in the Bible. In seven days the entire creation was completed including God's rest day. Man has seven needs, according to Maslow's theory of the hierarchy of needs.

There are seven days in a week. Joshua walked around Jericho seven times. In Egypt Joseph prophesied seven years of prosperity and seven years of famine. In the story of the feeding of the four thousand, Jesus used seven loaves of bread, and seven baskets of scraps were left over. The letter in Revelation was to seven churches.

There were seven lamp stands. And on it goes. Now it is our task to use the power of God to take over each of the seven mountains of the nation states.

As stated in the introduction, I will be interchanging the words *'mountains'* and *'sectors'* in the nations for ease of understanding. But the Bible uses the word *mountain*, so I will use more of that as we proceed.

"When the Lord your God brings you into the land which you go to possess, and has cast out many nations before you, the Hittites and the Girgashites and the Amorites and the Canaanites and the Perizzites and the Hivites and the Jebusites, seven nations greater and mightier than you..." Deuteronomy 7:1

The first enemy we have to overcome are the Hittites. I will explain what they represent in the next chapter and how they rule over the **media** sector.

Next are the Girgashites who represent corruption. They represent the satanic principality which rules the mountain of **government** and **politics**.

Next come the Amorites who represent humanism. They rule the mountain of **education**. Then the Canaanites, who represent the love of money, rule the mountain of the **economy** or **business**. The Hivites, who represent compromise, rule the **arts, fashion** and **entertainment**. The Perizzites, who represent idolatry, rule the mountain of **religion**. Finally we have the Jebusites who represent rejection. It is they who rule the mountain of **family**.

"And when the Lord your God delivers them over to you, you shall conquer them and utterly destroy them. You shall make no covenant with them nor show mercy to them." (Deuteronomy 7:2)

This was an instruction of God to the people of Israel before they could take the Promised Land. This means that in order for each one of us, and for the church as a whole, to enter into our spiritual inheritance, we must be able to overtake seven nations: the Hittites, the Girgashites, the Amorites, the Canaanites, the Perizzites, the Hivites, and the Jebusites.

These nations, which were in the past literal peoples, now represent seven "varieties" of evil spirits, which are the evil counterparts of the seven spirits of God (Revelation 3:1, Revelation 5:6, Zechariah 4:10).

Until we can overcome these seven mountains (or sectors) and reclaim them, we cannot possess the Promised Land and take the nations for God. Hopefully you are now beginning to appreciate more the task before the church of God.

We have a lot of work to do. Do you now see why playing "church as usual" is futile? Do you now see how playing the numbers game in churches is unhelpful if we do not equip and send out the believers to take these mountains? Sadly, some believers are directing their firepower towards each other rather than directing it towards the mountains.

Now we can see why the devil doesn't mind our remaining in our charismatic bubble, as long as we remain behind that small wall of the palace called Religion and allow Satan to hold sway and plunder every other mountain. He knows we will never be able to take the nations unless we come out of our charismatic ghetto.

This sad narrative is exemplified in the nation of Nigeria, where there are more churches per square mile than in any other country, and yet satanic spirits and the occult rule the people. Nigeria is the most churched nation, but also one of the most corrupt. This means the number of churches or Christians does not equate to righteousness, unless the Christians are trained and equipped to take these seven mountains for the Lord.

The church has been inward looking and introverted for too long. For many, sadly, it has been about the size of their churches, not about the impact they have made in their nations. That must change.

Now the question should be: which of these mountains are *you* reclaiming? This book will help you discover the mountain you have been sent to reclaim and how you can best do it. Be expectant and get ready to invade the territories of darkness with righteousness and dominion.

This is a collective task. It's not possible that you have been called to attack all these mountains by yourself, otherwise the rest of us might as well just close up shop. My prayer is that as you go through Part B of this book, you'll begin to locate which mountain is your own assignment. That will be a combination of your prayerful discernment of what God says you should do, plus the use of the skills and talents God has given you.

I will reveal to you the dominant satanic principality in each sector or mountain, as previously identified. So by understanding what the ruling spirits are, you'll be able to understand what you need to do to reclaim any of these mountains. Please note: You can never reclaim a mountain if the prevailing spirit over that mountain represents your area of current weakness.

For example, if you are slave to greed, and covetousness is your weakness, forget trying to take the mountain of economy. The Canaanites will floor you easily. But that doesn't mean you can't take the mountain of *family* or any of the others. This truth will become clearer as we proceed.

Despite this obvious truth, there are people in the church who still believe we should remain inward and not participate in civic life. I wonder what Bible they are reading! This division of life into spiritual and secular is wholly unscriptural. Everything we do, as humans, is spiritual — whether it's in the marketplace or in a building called church. We must grasp this if we are to confront the systems of Babylon and dislodge the strongman from the hill of God that became the garrison of the Philistines (1 Samuel 10).

For the kingdoms of this world to become the kingdom of our God and of his Christ, we must take over new frontiers. Our goal is to change the geography of the nations. The social sciences tell us there are certain parameters needed to define a nation's demography — the population mix, land mass, and so on. But God defines the demography of nations differently.

The spiritual climate of a nation affects the natural climate. So when God looks at any nation, he sees four categories of people that he holds responsible for its climate.

*"And the word of the LORD came to me, saying, ^{24}"Son of man, say to her: 'You are a land that is not cleansed or rained on in the day of indignation.' ^{25} The conspiracy of her prophets in her midst is like a roaring lion tearing the prey; they have devoured people; they have taken treasure and precious things; they have made many widows in her midst. ^{26} Her **PRIESTS** have violated my law and profaned my holy things; they have not distinguished between the holy and unholy, nor have they made known the difference between the unclean and the clean; and they have hidden their eyes from my Sabbaths, so that I am profaned among them. ^{27} Her **PRINCES** in her midst are like wolves tearing the prey, to shed blood, to destroy people, and to get dishonest gain.^{28} Her **PROPHETS** plastered them with untempered mortar, seeing false visions, and divining lies for them, saying, 'Thus says the Lord GOD,' when the LORD had not spoken^{29} The **PEOPLE** of the land have used oppressions, committed robbery, and mistreated the poor and needy; and they wrongfully oppress the stranger. ^{30} So I sought for a man among them who would make a wall, and stand*

in the gap before me on behalf of the land, that I should not destroy it; but I found no one. ³¹ Therefore I have poured out my indignation on them; I have consumed them with the fire of my wrath; and I have recompensed their deeds on their own heads," says the Lord GOD. Ezekiel 22:23-31 (NKJV)

The four categories of people that God holds responsible for the climate in every nation are:
- The Prophets
- The Priests *(pastors)*
- The Princes *(marketplace leaders in the seven mountains)*
- The People *(everybody else)*

As you see from the scripture, God holds us responsible for the climate in our nations. But more importantly, the nations can never be transformed if we abdicate our role in the marketplace, allowing the princes of darkness to rule.

We need to extend the frontiers of God's kingdom into the marketplace and reclaim the seven sectors (mountains) for him before we can see transformation in our cities and nations. It is unscriptural for any believer to think we should abandon the marketplace to the unrighteous. Such thinking merely perpetuates satanic dominance of the marketplace and handicaps the gospel's ability to entrench righteousness in our nations. Thank God, change is already happening.

In the beginning, after Lucifer and his cohorts were expelled from heaven they had no place where they could legally operate. So Satan was not interested in Adam and Eve as individuals. He was interested in the territory that was theirs so he could have a legal place to operate. From the beginning he was interested mainly in the territory called Earth.

When he got that territory, he spread himself across the seven mountains (sectors, as identified earlier) and now we're trying to reclaim those mountains from him so God's kingdom can rule on earth. The church has been focusing on the Religion sector, thinking it was a matter of loud shouts from the pulpit. But it's to the gates of the enemy that we need to take the battle.

Christians have discouraged participation in many areas of civic life in order to encourage "holiness." What foolishness! For example, for a long time (until recently) it was considered sinful by many in the church to get involved in the world of fashion, arts and entertainment. As a result of the long absence of light, darkness now dominates that sector, as we will see in a later chapter on this mountain.

People of unbiblical affinities now dominate the fashion industry, and in this sector belief in God has been almost erased from the hearts of many. We've left a whole swathe of the economy to the devil. If we don't engage with that mountain the enemy will put his own people there, as has happened for generations. Ironically, those same fashion designers that we abandoned now influence what Christian children wear.

Saving that which was lost
God's original plan in Genesis 1 was that human beings should exercise dominion over the earth. Dominion was lost in the garden, but Jesus reminds us Luke 19:10 that *"the Son of Man has come to seek and save that which was lost."* What was lost? Both animate and inanimate things.

In Colossians 1:19-20, we read:
For it pleased the Father that in him all the fullness should dwell, [20] *and by him to reconcile* **all things** *to himself, by him, whether things on earth or things in heaven, having made peace through the blood of his cross.*

He explains that "all things" mean "things on earth, or things in heaven." In other words,

Christ did not come just to reconcile people. He came to reconcile all things that were lost. What were they?

The first thing that was lost in the garden was our relationship with God. Adam and Eve were cast out of the presence of God, so Christ came to reconcile us to our Creator.

The second thing that was lost was our relationship with each other. We see the broken relationship between Cain and Abel, Adam and Eve. After we have been reconciled to God in Christ, we can be reconciled to each other.

The third thing that was lost was our relationship with the marketplace (the productive earth). The Bible tells us the ground was cursed. So Christ came to reconcile us so that the situation before the fall (man's dominion over all the earth) might be restored. But to do that, we have to reclaim the seven mountains (sectors) of the nation state that the enemy has since occupied.

For it was the Father's good pleasure...to reconcile all things to himself. –Colossians 1:19-20 (ESV).

In him we have redemption through his blood, the forgiveness of sins, according to the riches of his grace. –Ephesians 1:7 (NKJV)

Christ came to reconcile all things and not just all people. All things means everything: people, nations and the marketplace. Praise God!

To summarise the three dimensions of Christ's redemption:
- **Personal** — our relationship with God
- **Interpersonal** — our relationship with one another
- **The marketplace (earth)** — our reclaiming of dominion over all created things, represented by the seven sectors of the nation state. Hallelujah!

So there is a divine call to pulpit ministry. I understand that and so do you, but there's an equally divine call for all believers to the marketplace. That is the call for every one of us in the church. It's not just about the five-fold ministry gifts.

To recap: whenever God looks at the condition of a nation, he holds responsible four key people: the priests, the princes, the prophets and the people. The priest represents the church, the pastors and the ministry gifts. The princes are those with power and control in the marketplace.

The prophets are those with a prophetic ministry. And the people are everybody else.

This makes us all responsible.

Now you can see the foolishness of statements like: "I'm not called to ministry. The pastor is the one called to ministry, so let him do all the work."

We all have work to do. We keep saying we're in the last days, but we've been idle for too long. The marketplace is ripe and it is time we invaded it and reclaimed it for God.

Take some time to thank God for what you have read so far. Pray that he will increase your capacity to receive, to retain and to release in the days to come. Receive that grace now. Amen.

Note here your Key Learning Points from Chapter 5

CHAPTER 6

HOW DID WE GET HERE?

The essential question is: how did the church of Christ get to where it is now? How did we lose our influence in the marketplace? What beliefs, behavioural patterns and institutional habits have brought us to the edge of the precipice?

How did believers come to abandon such a vast terrain? It's an area Christians are not influencing, and yet decisions made in it affect a lot of the things we and our children do on a daily basis. After all, we don't live in an insulated world.

Our objective is stated in Habakkuk 2:14:
"that the earth shall be filled with the knowledge of the glory of the Lord as the waters cover the sea."

The kingdoms of this world will indeed become the kingdom of our Lord. In other words, there will be a reclaiming of the kingdom, but not while we're still idle in the marketplace.

How Christians lost the mountains
1. Separation from God
I'm talking about what happened in Eden. Remember, Satan was not really interested in Adam per se. He was more interested in the territory that was under Adam's control. When we disobeyed God in Eden, we lost our control over the earth.

That's how Satan acquired a new title as the ruler of darkness of this world. Through Adam's actions he acquired the title deeds of earth.

But restoration is possible.
"... if my people who are called by my name will humble themselves and pray and seek my face and turn from their wicked ways...., I'll forgive their sins and I will restore their land." (2 Chronicles 7:14).

2. Confusing the gospel of salvation with the gospel of the kingdom.
Misunderstanding these two dimensions of the gospel is a problem for many in the church. The gospel of salvation is comparable to crossing the *Red Sea*. The blood of Jesus frees us from our oppressor, the devil, who in this case can be compared with Egypt.

The gospel of the kingdom, the other hand, is represented by the crossing of the *Jordan*. To reach the Promised Land, we need to cross the Jordan after crossing the Red Sea. This means conquering seven hostile kingdoms before the land can be ours.

Many Christians focus on the gospel of salvation, and many churches seem more concerned with filling their pews on Sunday than with the biblical transformation of nations. The reality is, while many Christians are busy trying to get people into the church, the enemy is taking over every strategic area of our nation.

This is not to say anything is wrong with the gospel of salvation. It is a vital beginning. But stopping at salvation is like sitting down after crossing the Red Sea, or going no further than the edge of the Jordan. We are not taking territories or exercising dominion.

We need to transition from escaping from sin (the gospel of salvation) into occupying territories and nations for God. That's the part we have not done properly as the church. The early church transformed Israel, transformed the Roman Empire, and laid the foundation for the prosperity of Western and European nations.

The early Christians made an impact on

European history. Most of the founding fathers of America were Christians too. So Christians in the past have influenced nations and territories. But it seems that just a few generations later we retreated into our silos, ceding a whole sphere of influence to the enemy.

That period is now over, in Jesus name!
Some more examples: Salvation alone does not create a change in culture. We see examples of the gospel of salvation in countries like Nigeria, Kenya and Uganda, where there are plenty of churches and Christians and yet you cannot see the corresponding positive impact of the Christian faith on national culture and development.

By contrast, there is a town called Almolonga in Guatemala where 80 percent of the people are reported to be born-again Christians. Crime there is the lowest in the nation. Before revival reached the town, they had several jails and a high crime rate. I was told they had only one jail now because the other four were empty and had to be closed. That's how it should be!

The naivety and complacency of many in the church is reflective of the enemy's strategies. The Muslims are onto it. They are not content with just being Muslims. They want to Islamize any nation they are in, even a Western one.

They've decided that staying in their mosque and praying is not enough. They want to take over the nations.

Meanwhile church folk seem to be mainly interested in taking over the little piece of land called church. They exert no influence where it matters in their nation. This passive posture has to change. John the Baptist was not content to preach repentance to the peasants. He spoke the truth to the powerful. He was a thorn in the flesh of the establishment.

Muslims want to do more than build mosques. They want to control the nations they are in, in terms of the laws and the cultural values. That's the objective of fundamentalist Islam. By contrast many pastors are just interested in having 30,000-member churches that influence nobody's territory.

Change is here. We must take the good news and permeate entire territories with it in order to establish Christ's kingdom.

3. An unbiblical view of work and ministry

Many Christians feel that what they do in church on a Sunday is sacred but on Monday morning, when they get to work, that's secular. That's a lie from the pit of hell. The word "secular" actually means "without God." But truly nothing exists without God.

All things *were made through him, and without him nothing was made that was made. – John 1:3 (NKJV)*

We need to deal with this fundamental point and needful and paradigm shift. Everything we do in or out of "church" is spiritual in nature. This common misunderstanding about the sacred/secular divide leads to the situation where a sister leads praise and worship on Sunday morning, looking like an angel, and on Monday the same woman is in her office shouting and behaving like a devil.

In church many put on a garment of spirituality, but from Monday they live in a God-free zone. As Christ followers, we have a duty to be God's ambassadors everywhere we go.

Equality in Calling
Whether our calling is to the marketplace or the five-fold ministry should make no difference to our engagement in spiritual warfare. We will have satanic principalities to contend with regardless of our calling. This mistaken doctrine of the spiritual-secular divide was illustrated in the late 70s, 80s and 90s when many charismatic denominations encouraged their members who were high up in business world to

resign and come into what they called "full time ministry." What a catastrophic error!

During this period members who were bank managers were strongly persuaded to resign from their jobs and become full time pastors. I remember helping many who became destitute because the churches could no longer afford to pay for their lifestyle. What foolishness!

Imagine the influence those believers would have had in the marketplace as board level directors, had they remained in their jobs. There is nothing wrong with resigning your job to do church work full time, as long as it is the Lord who is directing you to do so. There is no substitute for obeying God.

For a long time there has been no understanding of the equality of calling in the church. There has been the perception that being called to the fivefold ministry is more commendable than being called into the marketplace. Yet the ministry as we know it cannot survive without the input of marketplace resources.

We need to embrace the proper definition of *ministry*. Many have been defining ministry purely as the fivefold ministry gifts in the church, not understanding that those called to the marketplace are also in ministry.

This is one of the reasons we lost the mountains. The local church has operated more like a cruise liner than a battle ship.

A recent survey I read concluded that 80 percent of believers felt that what they were hearing on Sunday did not prepare them for the reality of what they confronted at work. They wanted more practical and relevant training. This lack solidified in their minds the divide between ministry (spiritual) and work (secular). Is this the reality in your city and nation?

Satan does not mind the church organizing prayer conferences, spiritual warfare conferences, pastors and church unity gatherings, believers' conventions, holy convocations and festivals — as long as we do not disturb his hold on the marketplace.

Thank God that is about to change. Whenever God wants to influence a nation, one of the first things he does is to place his servant near a mountain of influence in that nation. This should tell us that we need to reclaim these mountains. We must engage personally and proactively with each of the mountains of culture and influence in the nation.

There are many biblical examples of this approach. How did God influence Egypt? He placed Moses near Pharaoh (to learn the secrets of the leadership in Egypt) and that led to the eventual deliverance of God's people.

When God wanted to influence another generation of Pharaohs, He raised up Joseph to sit next to the powers in the land. When God wanted to influence Babylon, he placed Nehemiah near King Artaxerxes, and what was the result? The wall was rebuilt.

In Babylon we also saw Daniel positioned strategically in the palace of king Nebuchadnezzar. Through Daniel, national influence was established.

Then God wanted to influence Persia from within. He placed another of his servants, Esther, near King Xerxes, and the Jewish nation was saved.

You can see the biblical pattern from these examples. When God wants to transform or influence any nation, he does not do this from a distance. He places his people strategically within the mountain to be influenced.

So there is a picture of how we are supposed to reclaim these seven mountains. It is not by

Christians staying in temples and praying for them even though that's good. No! We've seen that the only way is by physically being present near each mountain. We need to be engaged.

In Psalm 2:8 God said "Ask of me and I will make the nations your inheritance, the ends of the earth your possession."

STRATEGIC MISTAKES OF THE CHURCH
What are the strategic errors we Christians have made?

1. The prosperity gospel
Outside the context of "transforming nations" this drive for prosperity is as foolish as Israel expecting milk and honey in the wilderness. Outside the context of taking nations and territories, God will question why we want prosperity. What is the purpose? You want me to prosper you, but what for? So you can have a big house? So you can have a bigger church building?

God says he is not interested in these things. He wants to prosper us so that we can take the nations. Hallelujah! He knows more than anyone else that if purpose is lost, abuse is inevitable.

Rather than saying the message of prosperity is

wrong, let us say that Christians that have not developed the proper perspectives for it, so it looks wrong. The kingdom needs a prosperity revival now, as the challenges are many and the task of transforming nations is huge. That is why the Lord said in Zechariah 1:17 *"My towns will again overflow with prosperity."* Establishing his kingdom requires prosperity.

Do you know that there are some people on this earth who are so rich they can go to any nation, sponsor any candidate they want for the leadership and that candidate will win because he has huge financial backing? Can you imagine if that were a born-again Christian? Can you imagine a believer being as rich as Bill Gates and thus able to begin to influence nations?

It's very important that we start looking outward rather than inward. Christ is coming for his church! And he says the kingdoms of this world will become the kingdoms of our God. So he is coming to impact the entire territory as well. Hallelujah!

2. Wilderness and the promise of abundance don't go together

As believers we have lived in a Christian wilderness zone for a long time. What do I mean? We've left Egypt in the sense that we got saved, but we've not entered the Promised Land. Why? Because we have grown comfortable in the wilderness and we think God will give us milk and honey there. It will not happen. The church will never come into true abundance until we realign our purposes with God's and see the nations as our constituencies. Once we are focused on the extension of the frontiers of his kingdom, wealth will flow. We will be overwhelmed with resources, once purpose is established.

3. There is a limit to the power God will release to us if our goal is just to make the wilderness more liveable.
That's what believers have been doing for a long time now. We have not been seeking the Promised Land by trying to take nations for the Lord. We want to stay in our wilderness and make it more liveable. We want air-conditioning! We like the promise of milk and honey but we want it here, rather than going to where God wants us to get it from. We haven't understood the wilderness is just a transit lounge.

If you are a Christian who is engaged in the marketplace, **there are three stages of obedience** to becoming somebody who can influence your sphere for God. You develop a new mind-set. You begin with the gospel of salvation and then move to embrace the gospel of the kingdom.

1. *The stage of convenience*
"It is my business and I will do it my way." "I have a PhD in business and banking, so that is the way we do it." From here you have to be able to move to the next stage, which comes as you mature in God.

2. *The stage of crisis*
"My business, but his way"
In other words, it's still my business (Charles Omole Incorporated) but since my way has proved unproductive and limiting, maybe God's way will do the trick.

Here you will begin to ask, the Lord if he thinks you should do the business, and how you should do it. Your failures doing it your own way during stage one have humbled you and make you more open to God's input. But at this stage you still see the business as yours.

3. *The stage of conviction*
"His business, his way"
We now accept that God owns everything. We say, "God, this is *your* business." That is where we manifest his glory and develop the sensitivity to dominate in the marketplace.

We can see that as we move through these

stages, personal discretion begins to decrease. We begin to do more of what God wants and less of our own agenda.

It's not enough to have Christians on these mountains. We must be Christians with a culture-changing faith who can influence the sphere of our operation.

So what is the Great Commission? Matthew 28:19 says, *Therefore go and make disciples of all nations, baptising them the in name of the Father, and of the Son, and of the Holy Spirit.*

Now, how do you baptise nations? We can see that the word *nation* has multiple meanings. The plain meaning is a nation state as we know it, but embedded within that are the people who make up the nation, because it's people that we baptise. And as we do, we are immersing the nations in righteousness. So our objective has to be to possess the nations for God. That's why the Bible tells us to make disciples of all *nations*, not of all *souls*.

While we have been focusing exclusively on church membership, Lucifer's grip on the nations has strengthened.

Without opposition he has dominated the marketplace, the place we were supposed to have occupied. Remember Jesus' words when he was leaving us? *"...Occupy till I come..."*

But we have been occupying our church buildings instead, and the places we were supposed to have occupied we've left for the devil and his cohorts. Then we complain when the devil makes decisions that are not consonant with what we want as a church. It is time to change this reality by the force of righteousness.

Finally...
Beginning with the next chapter, we'll begin a sector by sector analysis of the marketplace. As I explained in the Introduction, as a result of Adam and Even's fall in Eden, Satan gained a new title. He became the ruler of the darkness of this world. But there is one thing you need to know about the way he operates.

Although he's a spiritual being, *Satan is not omnipresent.* That is, he can only be in one place at a time. He is not like God who is everywhere. Because of this limitation, Satan divided the earth and its sectors into territories. He then appointed his demons as territorial spirits to oppress and enforce his evil intentions in each sector (or mountain).

Occasionally Satan shows up in person in a

specific territory, if the issues are escalated to him. But he has appointed his most trusted demons to each of the seven mountains in the marketplace.

So we cannot make progress as Christians until we have developed the spiritual stature needed to overcome the principalities. Business is all about spiritual warfare, not our qualifications or contacts. As tools in Satan's hands, those who lack your qualifications can still become your bosses. So brace yourself!

Get ready to push into your destiny in God with the force of righteousness and the banner of love and grace. In the following chapters; we will now examine each of the sectors or mountains in some detail.

Note here your Key Learning Points from Chapter 6

CHAPTER 7
BREAKTHROUGH STRATEGIES IN THE <u>MEDIA</u> SECTOR

Mountain #1

The first sector or mountain we will examine is the **media**. From here on I will use the word "mountain" more, because of our reference text in Isaiah 2. It tells us the mountain of the Lord's house will be exalted "above all other mountains." "Mountain" also suggests an obstacle.

When the Lord your God brings you into the land which you go to possess, and has cast out many nations before you, the Hittites... **Deut.7:1**

The realities of the media mountain
Evil forces currently occupy this mountain almost entirely because the church has never recognized the value of taking it for the

kingdom. The media has become a major tool of the enemy, and we must get it back. Satan has lived almost unopposed on this mountain and taken full advantage of its influence. And the church has been a victim.

Media here refer to news outlets that report and establish the news. **The media do not just report news anymore, they create it.** If you are conversant with the media you'll know this is true. The media will send their reporters to snoop on people and pose as others in order to create news.

Before they just reported what happened. Now they engineer events to report on, and they give this news they create any spin they like. They can turn a non-story into a big story and make a big story a non-story.

The media here include TV stations and networks, social media and websites, blogs, newspapers, radio stations and magazines. One of the issues of the internet is that it is completely uncensored, so anybody can publish any falsehood they want on a website and it can become big news quickly.

So if your name or someone else's appears on a website, a whole load of people, especially younger ones, will assume it is true.

But not everything on a website is authentic. The Internet is widely abused because of the possibility of anonymity. You can get away with inventing anything you like about someone because it will be difficult to identify you.

So it's important you understand how powerful the media is worldwide.

Hittites rule the media mountain

Hittite comes from the name *Hit* which means fear or terror. Bad news is Satan's specialty, just as ours is good news. The media create fear and anxiety through their influx of bad news. The satanic principality that governs and rules the mountain of media is called Apollyon in Greek and Abaddon in Hebrew. It is mentioned in Revelation 9:11.

Its job is to destroy reputations, destroy confidence, destroy self-esteem, and destroy lives. It is a destroyer par excellence, and uses the media to decimate the aspirations of generations. Friends, the media is not as innocent as many of you think. It is a satanic tool that is shaping a whole generation.

The media will be a vital tool in the hands of the antichrist. This is why Satan has deployed his vicious principality to control it.

John Bunyan's classic allegory. *The Pilgrim's Progress,* includes a memorable scene in which Christian does battle with a demonic monster named Apollyon.

True to its name, Apollyon nearly destroys Christian. The pilgrim in his armour withstands the attack and wields his sword to repel the monster. Bunyan's "Apollyon" is a symbol of our spiritual enemy, but the inspiration for the character is literal.

The Abaddon/Apollyon of Revelation is a real being who, as one of Satan's henchmen, will one day inflict real pain on real people. For now he is driving the media mountain to achieve destruction.

Question: When was the last time you read or heard any bad news regarding the private life of Rupert Murdoch? If at all, it was reported in a banal way. Why are they not reporting on him? Because he is one of those who have a stronghold over the media in the UK, in the US, and in Australia.

So for every story you file about him he'll send his dogs to sniff out ten about you. Thus he's practically immune from criticism in terms of his private life. He may be criticised in a business sense, but the kinds of thing reporters do to other people such as enticing them with fake prostitutes, they'll never do with him.

Apollyon means destroyer or distraction. The name suggests fear or terror. This demonic influence can cause deception, lack of truth telling, manipulation of the truth or partial truth, and it can instil fear in society at large.

The media's power to control the narrative of what you believe as a Christian is overcome by a wholesome knowledge of the Word of God. Satan's deception will be so effective in the last days that Christians will need the utmost sensitivity if they are to discern the wheat from the tares.

Remember, the Bible says that if it were possible even the very elect would be deceived (Matthew 24:24). The deception will be so convincing that a casual observer will find it hard to spot the difference.

Satan knows this. That's why he seconded his most trusted demon as governor over this mountain. So ask yourself: What is the basis of your belief about the church? What is the basis for what your belief about pastors and money in the church?

Are these beliefs of yours based in Scripture or

the voice of God? Or are they based in what you have been told by the media?

You may be surprised that the media have dictated what many in the church believe. Having organised this, Satan can easily control the actions of Christians, and he will influence their individual wills to do this. I discussed this satanic deception in detail in my recent book titled *Getting the Story Straight*. To read more, get a copy.

The media can also shape culture so that it is viewed in an ungodly and humanistic way. Isn't that what they have been doing? We've abandoned the media, but it goes on influencing the nations.

Did you know that the dominant media in the entire Western world are controlled by fewer than a hundred people? These people in turn are being unwittingly controlled by Apollyon. Now you see why the media is more interested in bad news — the job of its prevailing spirit is to terrorise people.

Apollyon is a destroyer. His job is to create fear and change the culture of nations to advance Satan's agenda and destroy the church of the living God.

Many wonder why the media report bad news, but bad news sells more newspapers and magazines. So the people who criticise them are also guilty.

Over the years Satan has created an appetite for bad news in people, so that the media can make more money out of selling fear. This relationship with the media is vital because, sadly, many in church assume that whatever the media say must be true. Falsehood has become easier to sell than truth.

Satan uses the media to change the public discourse and opinion from time to time, to advance his agenda on the earth. An example of how the media has been used to change public opinion is the current debate about homosexuality in many nations. What used to be seen as deviant and immoral twenty five years ago has now become mainstream. Why? It is because of the media strategy employed by Apollyon and his agents. Let me quote from an article written by Os Hillman on this subject early in 2013:

MEDIA CASE STUDY: The Strategy of the Gay Agenda in America.
In February 1988, a meeting was held with 175 gay activists in Warrenton, Virginia. Marshall Kirk, a Harvard-educated researcher in

neuropsychiatry, and Hunter Madsen, who holds a doctorate in politics from Harvard and is an expert in persuasion tactics and social marketing, were the conveners of this meeting.

In their book, *After the Ball*, a strategic battle plan was outlined to make homosexuality acceptable in the minds of Americans. They said, *"AIDS gives us a chance, however brief, to establish ourselves as a victimized minority, legitimately deserving of America's special protection and care. AIDS generates mass hysteria of precisely the sort that has brought about public stonings and leper colonies since the Dark Ages and before. . . . How can we maximize the sympathy and minimize the fear? How, given the horrid hand that AIDS has dealt us, can we best play it?"*

This was the beginning of a public relations multi-year plan. They developed a public relations bible for the gay movement, and outlined the key strategies for the movement in their book.

Their goals included:
- To break current negative associations with our cause and replace them with positive associations.
- To change what people actually think and feel, by reframing the terms of the debate.

- To seek desensitization and nothing more (until it doesn't matter anymore).
- To make it unlawful to discriminate against gays.

Public perception of the gay agenda
Seventeen magazine has done a survey about the gay lifestyle for several years. To get an idea of how effective the gay rights movement has been with public relations, one only needs to look at this survey of its readers compared to earlier years. Consider their 1991 survey, which revealed that 17 percent of their readers accepted homosexuality as appropriate. In their 1999 survey, however, after *eight years of the PR and media campaign,* 54 percent of respondents accepted homosexuality as appropriate.

"I was born this way"
In 2011, pop artist Lady Gaga received three American Music Awards from three nominations for her smash hit "Born This Way." Millions of young people and adults under forty heard the gay propaganda over the airwaves, compliments of Lady Gaga.

CNN weekend anchor, Don Lemmon, revealed during an interview in 2012 that he was gay. During one of his interviews with someone else on a CNN broadcast he subtly commented to the interviewee that he knew he was born gay. Because of the power of media, viewers often take what is said as truth.

Our young people, especially, have bought this lie. Yet there is no scientific data that proves a person is genetically predisposed to homosexuality. This deception is promulgated in the media, with few willing to state the truth for fear of a backlash from the gay community.

Most of us hear from gay activists that they were born gay. They deny their sexual preference is a function of how they were raised or that exposure to societal factors and childhood wounds predisposed them to the lifestyle.

After the Ball authors Kirk and Madsen acknowledge in their book: *"We argue that, for all practical purposes, gays should be considered to have been born gay, even though sexual orientation, for most humans, seems to be the product of a complex interaction between innate predispositions and environmental factors during childhood and early adolescence."* Here is an amazing admission by gay leaders that they were not born gay.

What is their ultimate goal? It isn't just to get acceptance. David Kupelian explains: "The end game is not only to bring about the complete acceptance of homosexuality, including same-sex marriage, but also to prohibit and even criminalize public criticism of homosexuality. In other words, to jam criticism with the force of law. This is already the case in Canada and parts of Scandinavia."

[The above case study is an extract from an article titled: *Is Gay Marriage a Moral Issue or a Civil Liberties Issue?* by Os Hillman. Os is a great marketplace apostle].

FOUR KEY FEATURES OF SATANIC STRATEGIC CONTROL OF THE MEDIA SECTOR.

Media ownership

By ensuring his own people own the media businesses, Satan can control their focus and attention. The media has long abandoned the craft of simply reporting news. They now create it, to engineer their own outcomes.

The first strategy of Apollyon is to ensure all those who control the dominant media in the world are either people who overtly worship him through occultist and satanic groups, or those who unwittingly enable him to manipulate and control them. Hence it will be impossible today for a Christian to own any dominant media outfit without victorious spiritual warfare.

Agenda setting
Through his ownership of the media outfits, Satan sets the agenda that suits him, and he ignores the agenda that does not. That is why good news is ignored by the media and bad news is actively sought and promoted. Repeated exposure to a particular slant of news softens people up and makes it easier for them to be sold a lie. We saw that in the strategy employed by the gay movement in the US.

Seductiveness
The media encourages you to make choices without any moral consideration. This is done in advertising all over the world. For example, why is it necessary to use semi-naked women to sell cars? What has that image got to do with cars, except to promote greed, ego and pride? Seductiveness is one tool used by the media. The goal of the Hittite is to change people's understanding of their core beliefs and gradually break down any opposition.

Appeal to human senses and logic
Much of the work of the antichrist will be established through the acquiescence of most of the citizen. The use of logic and human sensibilities is vital here. Through the educational system influenced by Satan (we'll

discuss this more when we look at the education mountain), many have been conditioned to think in a particular way.

So when the government tells us that in order to reduce credit card fraud they will pilot a scheme whereby chips will be implanted in people's hands, enabling them to authenticate payments with their fingerprints, people agree. It does sound logical. But through such logic the infrastructure of the antichrist is being established on earth.

The media appeal a lot to our human emotions and use logic to warm us to their satanic agenda. But as Christians we are to think in line with Scripture. We do not have independent thoughts of our own. Something may make sense to me, but if it is not scriptural, I will not do it. Let God alone be true and every man (including you) be a liar.

I am asked if I agree with gay marriage. After all, they say, it is a matter of equality. As a trained lawyer I can understand that logic, and as a human being I agree. But I only think in accordance with Scripture and will defer to the Bible every time.

Therefore I am against gay marriage because the Scripture is against it. Pure and simple. To overcome this tactic of Satan we need to learn to overrule ourselves and allow only the will of God to stand. Do not allow human logic to dictate your actions. Base them only on the Word of God. This is critical to neutralising the deception orchestrated by Satan through the media.

How, as the Church, do we reclaim the media sector?

First of all we must collectively *repent*. We must stand in the gap just as Daniel and Nehemiah did. We must repent of the views we've had as a church, which have resulted in the abandonment of the marketplace to Satan. Pastors and leaders must repent of the ignorance that has insulated the church from its environment and caused the salt of the earth to remain in the salt-shaker.

We know the media have their satanic mandate and agenda. So they will not respond to the church just because we ask them. There are spiritual forces involved.

Secondly we need to become *prayerful*. Have you been called to this mountain? Decide this in your heart. Do you have what it takes? Are you good at writing stories? Are you gifted in broadcasting, social media, newspaper editing, journalism or mass communication? If so, then you and Christians with similar interests need to pray more about this sector of the marketplace. This is important because the media have become mouthpieces of Apollyon and Satan to frighten people needlessly.

Thirdly, we (collectively) need to *stand against the principality* (Apollyon). We need to develop back bones as Shadrach, Meshach and Abednego did. All those in the church who have been called into this mountain need to pray for boldness to say and do the right things.

Media manipulation is rampart worldwide, and we must act to end it. A small Christian network producer in the US was quoted recently as saying: "We need courage. What we speak and what we write shape reality or the perception of reality. It takes so much courage to actually push, agitate and stand for truth and righteousness."

We must pray that media practitioners develop the right attitudes and worldview that will enable them to stand amidst the evils that pervade the media world.

How do we reclaim the media sector as individuals?

We should personally *pray for the church to regain its biblical worldview.* Let this message and doctrine permeate all our churches in such a way that they will be able to understand their essential role in the redemption of the media mountain and the marketplace in general. We are the salt of the earth and the light of the world. Everything about us is about impacting the world. So as individuals we must stop being lights to the church alone. We're supposed to be impacting nations.

Secondly, in your own prayer times, both individual and corporate, remember journalists and others in the media. Pray that Christians among them will model what they really believe.

There may be some Christians currently working in the media who have not realised the vital role of journalism and the media as a ministry. It may be just a way to pay the bills. Because they have missed the ministry dimension, some Christians have actually written anti-Christian stories, not realising the satanic agenda at work. So pray for journalists and their needs.

Thirdly, individuals and local churches should spiritually adopt those in the media, especially if they live in cities where key national media are headquartered. This means individuals will develop a prayer list of top journalists and media personnel and begin to include them in their prayers, praying that God will begin to touch their hearts and turn them in the right direction. Pray for conviction to come upon those in the media who do not know God.

Fourthly, pray for the few Christians in the media, that God will grant them a spirit of boldness, like Shadrach, Meshach and Abednego who refused to worship the god of Babylon. It is possible to refuse to worship the god of Babylon and live to tell the story. This is what believers in this sector need to be told.

Fifthly, you as an individual should take an interest in the media world generally. Develop spiritual insight into its stories. This will enable you to see the spiritual "hands" behind many of the stories that come up day after day.

The media publish lies and deception every single day, as part of an overarching agenda sponsored by the ruler of the darkness of this world, Satan. We must not fall for his deception. Satan wouldn't know how to tell the truth even if he wanted to. Lies are embedded in his DNA.

As a result he has sold you many lies about yourself. Moreover, many Christians are now living their lives based not on what the word of God says about them but on what the enemy has told them through the media.

The enemy mounts a massive misinformation campaign against every believer. His job is to lower your self-esteem, kill your spirit, dampen your enthusiasm, and thwart every effort at personal achievement in your life. When the serpent went to the garden, he sold a lie to the woman. And the woman still believed him— can you imagine! Satan told her, "Don't mind God's instruction not to eat of that tree, because God knows that the day you eat it you will become like him."

But we know that in Genesis 1:26 God had already said, "Let us make man in our own image." So what was this woman sold? A big lie! Understand that a credible misinformation campaign is always based on partial truth. That is, it is not necessarily completely manufactured. It usually has five percent, ten percent, twenty percent of truth in it. That morsel of truth is then mixed with the big lies to help make them credible.

If you can agree with the tiny percent of the story that happens to be true, you then lower your guard and may be sold on the remaining ninety percent which is not. If everything were patently false, it would be harder for that story to stand. So scrutinise the media and understand it as an instrument used by Satan which Christians must take over and use for kingdom advancement.

Sixthly, pray for doors to be opened to godly men and women to become influential in the media. Those who are ready to do things God's way need favour.

Seventhly, consider going into the media sector if you feel led to do so. Christians should take steps to own media-related businesses. In addition to all the prayers, we must act physically to possess naturally what we have been given in the spirit. It's a combination of prayer and strategies that will enable us take this mountain.

The higher you go on this mountain, the stronger the demons that will be are assigned to you. This is classic spiritual warfare. Apollyon will not deal directly with small players in this sector. He will leave those jobs to his junior demons. But he will step in directly if you become a major player and influencer in the media.

In 1 Corinthians 9 we read: *"For a great and effective door has been opened unto me but there are many adversaries."* Of course, as more doors open you'll encounter more adversaries too.

Levels of engagement

There are three activities and influence levels of this and every mountain —low, intermediate and top levels.

In this case the low level is the media outlet or local newspaper. The intermediate levels are media outlets with regional and national distribution.

At the top of the mountain sits Apollyon himself. He directs the message and values of the national and global media because these are the ones that change global views.

The dominant ministry office that will engage with the media mountain are the evangelists. They will need the media to be under kingdom control to reach all nations with the gospel, as the Bible commands.

So we must continue to pray for God to raise people with evangelistic grace who will wage a holy war against Apollyon and his control of the media.

Note here your Key Learning Points from Chapter 7

CHAPTER 8

BREAKTHROUGH STRATEGIES IN THE <u>GOVERNMENT</u> ARENA

Mountain #2

Let us now look at the second mountain (or sector) that constitutes the marketplace — the mountain of *government*. After the Hittites the next tribe mentioned is the Girgashites, and you will recall that the Revelation 5:12 key that the Lamb is worthy to receive is *power*.

When the Lord your God brings you into the land which you go to possess, and has cast out many nations before you, the Hittites and the Girgashites and the Amorites and the Canaanites and the Perizzites and the Hivites and the Jebusites, seven nations greater and mightier than you... **Deut 7:1**

A colony of heaven

In thinking about this mountain we need to understand that the earth is a colony of heaven. When we look at God's original intention when he made the earth, we will understand our imperative to reclaim this mountain for the Lord.

A colony does things the way its colonial masters do in their home country. So if we look at Anglophone countries we see they have a lot of things in common with Britain because Britain once colonized them. Lawyers in Britain wear wigs and long gowns in cold weather.

In countries that were former colonies they still wear wigs and gowns, even though the weather is hot. That is the power of colonial influence.

Since the earth is a colony of heaven, we are supposed to do things on earth as they are done in heaven. Why is this important? At the end of colonial rule comes independence, and in Eden Adam declared his independence from heaven.

As a result of Adam's declaration of independence, the way God wanted the earth to be fashioned, structured and governed was no longer happening. Instead Satan became the ruler of the darkness of this world.

Once a colony declares independence, it can begin to move away from the style of its colonial master, and that's what happened to Adam.

For unto us a Child is born, unto us a Son is given; And the government will be upon his shoulder. And his name will be called Wonderful, Counsellor, Mighty God, Everlasting Father, Prince of Peace. ⁷ Of the increase of his government and peace there will be no end. Upon the throne of David and over his kingdom, to order it and establish it with judgment and justice from that time forward, even forever. The zeal of the Lord of hosts will perform this. –Isaiah 9:6-7

The Bible says the government will be upon the Lord's shoulder. He is bringing a new style of governance to earth to reclaim and establish the mountain of government. Hence the need reclaim what the enemy has taken.

In respect of the Girgashites and the mountain of government, as with the media, the church has virtually given up this important territory to the enemy. Even worse, many people in the church feel pastors should not speak about politics or government.

Better stick with the ministry, they say, in clear contradiction to our scriptural mandate to reclaim this mountain for God.

We have allowed fear to quench ambition and keep us from the positions God has destined for us as the church. The top of this mountain is occupied by a relatively small number of people. A tiny proportion of the overall population controls the politics of nations.

The strategic importance of government
Government can be defined as a political institution that rules a land and administers civil decency and justice at multiple levels. The name **Girgashites** means those who dwell in clay soil. They represent those who are motivated by earthly desires and ambitions, and the corruption brought on by the pride of life. Corruption is the impairment of integrity, virtue and morality. Most politicians are motivated by earthly desires and ambition.

This mountain is strategic since the laws it makes can affect every other mountain (sector) in the marketplace. That is why the evil ruler over this mountain is Lucifer himself. Knowing its strategic importance, he has decided not to allow any of his henchmen to control it.

This explains the bloody and brutal nature of politics in many nations. Now you understand why people are willing to kill to gain or keep political power. Satan attracts to himself all manner of evil practices. That is why almost all those in political power in the nations have satanic spiritual links.

The motivation of these satanic agents in politics is not money. Money may have been the initial driver, but it becomes an issue of *power*. This is why people kill to remain in political power, despite having billions in their accounts. They are wielding power on behalf of Lucifer to whom many have sworn allegiance. All the other mountains can be controlled and influenced from this vantage point.

Lucifer will keep his own people in government because he knows whoever controls the government stands a good chance of being able to control the other sectors of nations as well.

Legislators can create a rule today that changes everything. For instance, twenty years ago in most countries, being gay was practically illegal. Now luciferian governments full of gay people have come to power and have begun to change the laws of nations. As a result homosexual marriage is being legalised in nation after nation.

Yet the church has neglected this crucial mountain, opting instead for prayer meetings and conferences. Satan is happy for us to hold our believers conventions, because we are leaving him to occupy the more strategic places, and offering him no competition.

A good friend of mine suddenly developed a brain tumour and died few years ago in England. While I was praying for her, on learning she was ill, I told her something the Lord had revealed to me. She told me I was actually the third person with the same revelation.

She had been perfectly healthy, with no history of cancer in the family and nothing that pointed to it. The day she collapsed, which led to the tumour being found, was exactly three days after she publicly declared in the media that she would be standing as a local MP against a long-standing Member of Parliament in London.

She was the head of the local churches' leadership forum, so she could easily have mustered the votes of all the folks in the churches and won. She was a formidable challenge to the sitting MP who had been in office for more than twenty years. But three days after this public challenge she collapsed.

I told her that when she went into battle, she had not girded her loins. She did not bind the strongman, yet wanted to take his spoil. Satan fired at her before she could successfully dislodge one of his own. Friends, we must know that politics require spiritual power. The worst of humanity can be revealed in the area of government, as Satan rules it with a strong hand.

You have to be prepared for that battle. That is why any Christian who enters the mountain of government and is not spiritually strong will be brought down. Satan is entrenched over this mountain, as the usurping prince over the nations.

Manipulation and pride are his key instruments. His role over the nations is to stir up whatever will defeat the purposes of God on the earth. So God's purpose on earth will be difficult to accomplish if believers don't take the mountain of government.

How can the kingdoms of this world become the kingdoms of our God and of his Christ if the governments are controlled by Lucifer? Are you beginning to get this message? As believers we cannot think our responsibility is about a building called church. Our responsibility is to take over the mountains of national culture — the marketplace.

Girgashites and the mountain of government
When Satan, the antichrist, is ruling over this mountain, it will manifest in certain distinctive ways. Some of them are:

1.   *Working to destroy Israel*
The physical Israel (although we are the spiritual Israel) still has a place in God's plan. So working for the destruction of Israel (Numbers 23:23, Romans 11:1-36) is one of the key aims of the antichrist. The more nations Lucifer controls, the more he will work for the destruction of Israel. It's important for us to see this.

2.   *Working to destroy the next generation*
This is done by creating the legislative and judicial framework to support rampant abortion. Over the years abortions laws have been diluted in all the nations. Even countries like Ireland that once had strict laws against it have now relaxed the rules.

Wars are also tools in this agenda. Everybody knows the main victims of wars are children. Generations are decimated by wars and orchestrated destructions. We have countries in Africa that can hardly feed their people. Yet they spend money on machine guns.

For instance; In Nigeria, where the power

supply is not guaranteed for even two hours a day, they have paid billions to launch a satellite into space. That's what happens when the devil is ruling.

Does the idleness of the church in the marketplace embarrass you? As Christians we cannot afford to remain behind our four walls called church, thinking that what happens in our government doesn't matter. It does matter and we are supposed to invade and reclaim this arena with the force of righteousness.

3.   *Working to destroy Christianity*
We see this in the problems people have being Christians in supposedly Christian nations. Under the false banner of equality, other faiths (especially Islam) will begin to exert pressure outside the normally recognised Islamic countries.

Practising your faith as a Christian will begin to be challenged by governmental equality legislation all over the world. Political leaders in Christian nations will increasingly yield to the satanic agenda, under pressure from Lucifer and his agents, and — desperate to retain power — many politicians will do his bidding.

The drive to Islamise traditionally Christian nations will increase through governmental legislation and programmes. But we can reverse this trend by taking over this mountain top for the Lord.

The dominant spiritual office sent to take over this mountain of government is the Apostle. I don't just mean those who have the title "apostle" after their name. I am talking of those who have apostolic grace and anointing.

In fact, such people don't generally wear the title of "apostle" visibly, because one of their predominant characteristics is humility. True apostles, and those with apostolic grace, play a key role among those who will take over this mountain of government.

Apostles understand the power they carry, so they don't talk frivolously. When they say something will happen, it will happen. The apostle doesn't mind going unrecognised by the world because he or she is recognised where it matters — in heaven.

The displacement of Lucifer is guaranteed by God, and nation after nation will be pulled out of his clutches. In Isaiah chapter 14:12-16 (NLT) we read:

"How you have fallen from heaven oh shining star, son of the morning; you have been thrown

down to the earth, you who destroy the nations of the world. For you said to yourself, I will ascend to heaven and set my throne above God's star, I will preside on the mountain of the gods, far away from the north, I will climb to the highest heaven and be like the most high. Instead you will be brought down into the place of the dead down to its lowest depth. Everyone there will stir at you and ask, can this be the one who shook the earth and made the kingdoms of this world to tremble?"

It is clear there will be a dethroning of Lucifer. We see in the bible that Daniel, Esther and Joseph all had the apostolic grace to function in and to influence the governments where they lived. They show you different levels of involvement, because in Esther's case she was actually in the same bedroom as the king. This means our involvement in the mountain of government could be of three different types:

First is the *active* engagement where Christians will take part in politics, armed with the force of righteousness. We can enforce Christ's victory over Satan by becoming part of the political class. This is exemplified by Joseph as the prime minister of Egypt.

Next is the *strategic* participation, which will see Christians as advisers, strategist, mentors, political experts and technocrats. This platform was exemplified by Daniel. He was not a politician himself but he had the ear of the king.

The third and final platform is *private and personal* participation through direct political activism and the exercise of our democratic right to vote. This is the least to be expected of any believer. This level also includes Christians who are involved in the private lives of political players. Esther exemplified this. She had influence on the king through private access.

I am not exhorting you to become a political candidate if that is not your calling. You could be a mentor to politicians. You could have their ears, and they could listen to your counsel. That is how the influence happens.

Levels of participation
There are three levels of governmental participation: the top, the intermediate and the low levels of the mountain. The low level, of course, is the local and municipal level; the intermediate is the state and subnational level; and the top is the level of national and international leadership.

The top of the mountain should be the ultimate objective, as that is where Lucifer himself is entrenched. We must dislodge him.

What do we need to do?

The mountain of government is so expansive that it will be impossible for me to set out in one book all the strategies the Lord has revealed to me. Some of these are so potent that I will never put them in a book. They will be for direct action as we engage the political arena.

There is a uniqueness about the mountain of government because Lucifer himself is in charge. It is probably the only mountain God has reserved some "peculiar strategies" for. So God will show you particular ways of operating, depending on the reality of your location in the nations of the earth.

What must we do to reclaim this mountain? There are many strategies, and as I said, I won't put all of them writing, lest Lucifer find out what is coming to him in due season.

The following list is not exhaustive.
- *Be politically engaged* — at the very least, vote. This means reading the manifestoes of the parties and making a decision as the Lord leads you.
- *Prayerfully determine if you have the apostolic grace* concerning this mountain. Do you have the calling to politics and government? If so, it is time to act.

- Prayerfully determine if God wants you to *support existing or emerging righteous politicians* or join their ranks. In other words, your prayer should not just be, *Should I be a politician?* It could also be, *Whom should I support, of those already out there?*
- *Support good politicians* with funding, counsel or material support. Start donating to politicians whose causes you believe in. This can give you access that will give you influence.
- *Beware of and avoid strategies of the flesh,* because many people are engaging in these wrongly. God will reveal strategies and engagements at all levels; Satan is good at deception, so don't be fooled. Abraham in haste created Ishmael. This was a man-made strategy because he thought God's strategy was too slow. Don't rely, then, on carnal considerations. Let God light your way.

So how do you know your strategy as an individual to reclaim this mountain is from God? The answer is simple. *A God-given strategy for anything on this mountain will always carry some element of the impossible in it.*

Any strategy to reclaim this mountain will seem, when you look at it on paper, impossible. Because Lucifer is personally in charge of this mountain; you *must* get heaven's green light and strategies before you proceed. Otherwise Satan will flog you quickly.

Nothing about this mountain is straightforward. So if your strategy is entirely plausible and easy, it's probably not of God. God's strategy will always require the activation of faith. It's impossible to access the supernatural realm without that.

Our prayer must be accompanied by action steps, for faith without works is dead.

In the days and weeks to come I will be spending more time counselling and mentoring believers who have been called to the political and governmental arena. This chapter is just a tip of the iceberg as I plan to write a book entirely dedicated to this mountain in the season ahead.

Note here your Key Learning Points from Chapter 8

CHAPTER 9

BREAKTHROUGH STRATEGIES IN THE <u>EDUCATION</u> SECTOR

MOUNTAIN #3

The tribe that corresponds with the Mountain of Education are the Amorites. In Proverbs 4:7, we read: *"Wisdom is the principal thing. Therefore get wisdom. Thought it cost all you have, get understanding".*

"When the Lord your God brings you into the land which you go to possess, and has cast out many nations before you, the Hittites and the Girgashites and the Amorites... seven nations greater and mightier than you". **Deut.7:1**

Now who rules this mountain? The Amorites are the tribe equivalent to those who rule the mountain of education. The Amorites in Deuteronomy 7 were warlike mountaineers whose name meant *to boast or take pride in one's art*. The Amorite spirit was one of self-exaltation. The word for Amorite, in Hebrew, comes from another Hebrew word, *amar*, which means to utter or to say. This implies that people with Amorite spirits are people who want their names mentioned. They seek fame, human glory and greatness.

Amorites are descendants of Canaan, as we see in Genesis 10 and 1 Chronicles 1. They were a large and powerful nation who controlled much of the Promised Land (Joshua 10:5). They despised God's goodness and longsuffering by refusing to repent of their sins. So we can understand how the Amorites have become entrenched in this mountain and try to negate what God is doing.

Also, the satanic principality that rules over the mountain of education and commands the Amorites is a demon called *Beelzebub*. His name means "lord of the flies," representing the lies he tells. He is a Baal of lies, the chief lieutenant of Lucifer. He may even be another face of Satan himself, but he's clearly the right-hand demon of Lucifer, along with Apollyon. His tool for the advance of this mountain is lies and deception.

So Beelzebub is an expert at lying, but as I

stated in an earlier chapter, lies that are sold to people tend to have a tiny bit of truth mixed in. (If the lies were blatant, most people would see through them.)

*Then the disciples came to Jesus privately and said, "Why could we not cast it out?" So Jesus said to them, "Because of your unbelief, for assuredly, I say to you, if you have faith as a mustard seed, you will say to this **mountain**, 'Move from here to there,' and it will move; and nothing will be impossible for you."* –Matthew 17:19-20

When the Lord talks of our moving mountains, he is not just referring to big problems, as most of us assume. He is talking about uprooting spiritual powers in high places. So instead of focusing on getting things from God, our faith needs to focus on the tearing down of principalities and powers that get in the way of God's kingdom being established on earth.

We are soldiers in a battle to take back the earth for God. We are here not to please ourselves but to execute the orders of our Commander-in-Chief, the Lord Jesus Christ.

Taking back the earth's education from the Amorites will not be done through human means. It will be done through the activation of a faith that is apparently small in comparison to these spirits. But it has the dynamite potential to overtake them, because our faith is a seed with kingdom potential in it.

The first question is, what is education? It is *knowledge or a skill obtained or developed by a formal or informal learning process.* That is, you don't have to go to formal university or a more formal school in order to be educated.

Back in Africa, when people use the word "uneducated" they mix it with the word "illiterate," which means "unable to read or write." But being illiterate is not the same as being uneducated, although there is some crossover. Many of the local market women in Africa are educated even if they are not literate in the way we understand it.

That's why a definition of education has to include both the formal and the informal kind. In this chapter, we will be emphasising the formal education sector. After all, in most societies children are required by law to be educated to secondary school level. This is known as compulsory state education. But are governments doing this out of altruism or does this compulsion have ulterior motives?

The story from the government's side is that

compulsory education increases the life chances of every child. This may be true, but there are some key shortcomings based on the demonic spirit that controls the mountain of education, represented by the Amorites.

The earliest educational institutions had the goal of training and admonishing students in the fear of the Lord. That is why Christianity was at the forefront of education in earlier times. We see this in the names of public educational institutions that had Christian ministers as their heads, from Harvard, started by John Harvard, to Yale and Princeton. All were started by Christian mission groups. Their instruction was given in the context of a worldview that put God at the centre of life.

If you look at most good schools, even in the developing countries of Africa, they were initially Christian. So Christianity and education have always gone together for the advancement of society. Even today if you analyse the educational landscape of the United Kingdom, you will find that of the top one hundred primary and secondary schools in Britain, eighty per cent are church schools. There is something about an education reflecting God's worldview that makes it an ideal model.

Sadly, over the years the liberals have taken

over these institutions in such a way that God has been driven out of schools as Satan gets more desperate to control the narrative. A survey I was reading last year said that in the top five universities in the USA more than 79 per cent of the tutors considered themselves to be liberals. When the group was narrowed down to the top Ivy League schools, the liberal percentage was more than 90 per cent.

The schools' founders will be turning in their graves to see these schools built with Christian funds and based on Christian principles now being taken over by godless liberals who are beating the drum for the enemy's agenda. These top schools are now churning out liberally educated people who question everything about God.

The Free State education conspiracy
The history of compulsory state education around the world has been well documented, but modern European history suggests this policy has been a way to control the population and mould the thinking of its citizens. The first European to venture into this system was King Frederick William I of Prussia (now Germany) in the 1700s.

King William suffered a thumping defeat during the Napoleonic wars. With his army decimated, he faced the dilemma of how to maintain order in his kingdom without the military. He was advised he could strengthen the state's hold on the people through a system of compulsory, free state education.

With penalties for defaulting parents, children up to age fourteen had to attend state-run schools whose objective was to indoctrinate them and turn out obedient, loyal subjects. So it became easier to keep the peace without the need for a powerful military. The children were taught unquestioning loyalty to the king and service to the country. It worked.

The state groomed the children for a life of loyal service to the monarch. Sadly, in this regard little has changed from the 1700s. The state is still interested in turning out children who fit a particular mould, and in harassing non-conformists.

The state education system is mostly tasked with producing cheap labour for the government and the rich. That is why entrepreneurship is not the focus of state education in many nations. This deception is symptomatic of the satanic infrastructure in education.

How do we take over?
First, a spiritual takeover will begin in the

mountain of education if we can confront some "ism." Here are examples:

Atheism: This is the belief that there is no God. Half of the liberals in the top schools in the US call themselves atheists. They are people who are now ruled by their knowledge, by the facts they know. The Bible says, "The fool says in his heart there is no God." So with all their facts and education they are still fools.

Humanism: This rejects all dependence on faith, the supernatural or divinely revealed truth. Humanism places a premium on intellect and human qualities. It often manifests itself in rhetoric. That's why Paul said the gospel did not to people in enticing words of man's wisdom, but as a demonstration of Spirit and power. In other words, there are ways people can put words together that make you feel okay, but because these words are not rooted in the Word, they do not really change your life.

Rationalism: This is when logic rules a person. Rationalism means everything must make sense in the natural before you can accept it. But you and I know that if we applied rationalism to the Word, we would not believe anything. If I asked you if you had been born again and you said yes, how would you prove it? How do you prove to somebody outside yourself that you have been born again? You cannot. There's a knowing in your inner being that cannot be evidenced empirically. So if you are welded to rationalism it becomes difficult to live by faith.

Liberalism: This is seen in moral standards that fit the preferences of individuals, rather than being considered objective. In other words, you can do whatever you like as long as it you don't hurting anybody else. A result of liberalism is a hedonistic lifestyle. This has led to all kinds of unthinkable sexual activities, even bestiality where people get gratification from sex with animals. That is liberalism.

It also gives rise to the swingers. Swingers have partners — some are even married — but they are not monogamous. They swap partners, and even organise parties to facilitate the exchange. So liberalism has allowed much evil to flourish in the name of consensualism and freedom. Under liberalism, right and wrong are shifting sands. What was right ten years ago could be wrong today. What was wrong ten ago could be right today, so you never know where you stand. Everything depends on whims or opinion polls.

Liberalism also provides political cover for atheism and humanism. There are many liberal-leaning political parties in most of our countries, who are advancing these objectives. And these are the prevailing influences on global education.

As I said earlier, Beelzebub is the principality controlling the mountain of education. Let us see something interesting in the book of Daniel:

Then he said, "Do you know why I have come to you? And now I must return to fight with the prince of Persia; and when I have gone forth, indeed the prince of Greece will come –. **Daniel 10:20**

Daniel 10 gives us a fascinating glimpse into a spiritual world we do not ordinarily see. Certain characters are mentioned.

The first is the messenger angel who comes to bring the interpretation of Daniel's vision in Daniel 10. He is not named in this particular passage. Then there is the prince of Persia, evidently a fallen angel working under the direction of Satan who operates as "the god of this world" (2 Cor, 4:4).

The prince of Persia had withstood the messenger angel for twenty-one days and hindered him from coming to Daniel (as noted in Daniel 10:13). Also mentioned is Michael, one of the chief princes or what is called an "archangel." Michael comes to the rescue of the messenger angel and relieves him for a time so that he might bring the interpretation of the vision to Daniel.

In Daniel 12, Michael is called "the great prince who protects your people." So Michael the archangel came to the rescue because the Prince of Persia was too strong for the messenger angel.

Then the prince of Greece, another of Satan's mighty princes, like Beelzebub, is mentioned. Once Michael has gone, the prince of Greece will come. His coming is prophesied by the messenger angel. Later, Greece would become the dominant world empire.

Interestingly, much of the knowledge we use today emanated from Greece, the home of Plato and Aristotle. The Bible talks about the prince of Greece who came to dominate. The Greek education and belief systems eventually permeated the whole world.

It's important for us to understand the spiritual dimensions to what we do. Many of us don't question what we do because we don't know the root of it. After Greece became the main world empire, the rest of the world took its example and standards from it. This is the root of what we confront today in education.

What is the dominant ministry gift assigned to conquer this mountain of education? Of course it is the *teachers*. There has to be grace on their life to teach, and I'm not referring to the fivefold ministry gifts alone. Beyond the spiritual gift of teaching there has to be the grace to teach generally.

For example, I might have a prophetic grace from time to time but that doesn't make me a prophet by calling. I might have an evangelistic grace from time to time, but it doesn't make me a full-blown evangelist. My point is that we cannot confront this mountain without having some teaching grace in our life.

Some will be teachers by ministry gifts, some will not. It's not just about being a teacher of the Word. To confront this mountain we must be confirmed and empowered by the Holy Spirit. These Spirit-led teachers must understand that their role is to instruct in the way of the Lord, not just in the church but in the wider educational system.

What do Christians need to do to reclaim this mountain?
First we need teachers (not just with a ministry gift but generally speaking) that are equipped

with the Holy Spirit and ready to instruct in the way of the Lord.

Secondly we need to change the education curriculum. There must be more faith-shaping and God-centred materials in our schools. This is a major battle in the USA, for example about what goes into the curriculum. Unlike the UK, the US doesn't have a federal, top-down curriculum for schools, so each education board can determine what to include or exclude. There may be some basic standards across all schools, but boards have a lot of discretion in terms of the books they accept.

The liberals, for example, who will not allow the Bible or any Christian book to come into school, will allow books on witchcraft like the Harry Potter series. Even though such books appear to be innocent fun, those who know about spiritual operations will tell you that many of the depictions in these books are the actual modus operandi of satanic worship. The question has to be asked: how did the authors know these detailed secrets? Could they just be products of their innocent imaginations, or are they being fed by spiritual alliances unknown to many unassuming readers?

To bring change, Christians will need to strategize to get onto governing and management boards and to hold leadership positions in the administration of schools.

Either way, we need to get involved in shaping the educational policies of our nations. While we may not be able to influence curriculum, in some places being a member of a governing body gives you room to make some impact.

Levels of Engagement
As with the other mountains, this mountain has three levels. Lower down the mountain we need to fill teaching positions. Then there are the middle and top of the mountain in terms of the policy-makers and those who actually decide what is taught in schools and what books are read. You will be surprised at how a generation can be completely brainwashed by the educational system.

There are books that have slanted history, and as a result a whole generation of people have believed in an error. So it's important for us to understand that a generation can be shaped by lies if we don't get involved.

Prayer is vital to our victory also. We must get Christians with this revelation to penetrate everything that has to do with education in our nations. That's why we have to take over the mountain of education from all three levels. This is the thing I want you parents in particular to pay attention to:

Philippians 2:5 says, *"Let this mind be in you which was also in Christ..."* This means it is possible to have other kinds of minds in us. God would not say "Let this mind be in you" if there were no alternatives.

LEFT v RIGHT BRAIN ANALYSIS

When a child is born, they are born with both left and right brain competencies by default. The cerebral cortex of the left and that of the right link to the nervous system, and this is what processes information in the body.

We are all born with left and right brain processors. The way the left brain processes information and the way the right brain processes information are completely different. Stay with me here, because this is key.

Beelzebub and the Amorites have had us living and experiencing education through the left brain grid only. That is the goal of the formal education system in our societies which emphasizes the left brain grid and almost dumbs down the right brain element. When a child is born they are normally inclined towards right brain processing. That doesn't mean left brain is wrong. It means left brain is supposed to be ruled by right brain, so left brain is supposed to be subjected to the right brain processor.

Left brain processes words, right brain processes pictures in terms of language. Left brain is analytical, right brain is intuitive. When you know some things but can't explain them, that's your right brain. Whereas with left brain 1+1 must be 2, the right brain is more analytical. In terms of time, the left brain is sequential and the right brain simultaneous.

Some people who are right-brain oriented tend to lose their sense of time quickly because they are focused on what they are doing and time is less of an issue, though left brain is there to balance it. The basic question for the left brain person is *what*, whereas for the right-brain person it is *why*.

What is the question children ask while they are growing up? It's not *what*, but *why*. That's because by default every child has both left and right brain processors but at birth they incline more to the right brain.

What the formal education system then does is force them along the narrow part of the left brain analysis, only because Beelzebub needs that to control them.

Einstein was summarily expelled from school because he was considered to be disruptive. He wasn't. He was just too brainy. So there's a mould that society has created through the education system, and if your child doesn't fit squarely into it, they begin to call your child all kinds of names. Then you too begin to worry needlessly.

Upon entry into school, most children are predominantly right-brain processors or thinkers because that's the birth default. The education system forces them to conform to left-brain thinking only. That's part of the formal education system.

After a few years of formal education, and by the time children are in year three or four of primary education, most will have become left-brain dominant because of the way they are taught. They are forced to be purely logical. Intuitiveness and creativity can be easily lost.

By the time most children finish secondary education they will be left-brain dominant, and of course the higher they go in formal education the more entrenched they are in left-brain processing. So by the time they have a Masters and PhD, they are almost 100 percent left-brain led.

I must repeat that there is nothing wrong with left-brain processing. God gave us both left and right brains and both must be used. I am simply saying the default educational system favours left-brain logical processes at the expense of the more intuitive and perhaps illogical right-brain processing.

It could also be that parents need to help their children develop right-brain processing to balance the necessary left-brain inclination of the state education system. It could be argued that the state needs the left-brain bias to mass-produce educated children on the cheap; rather than the more expensive, individualised, right-brain development.

That is why most IQ and scholastic aptitude tests measure only left-brain skills. They are measuring objective skills. The point I'm making is the left brain quadrant makes it difficult to think out of the box.

Parents must do a lot to help and support their children in developing their right-brain quadrant. Children must be taught and encouraged to believe and develop faith in God intuitively. And parents should not accept just any label given to their gifted children by the educational system. If your children are outside the box, it does not mean there is a problem. You must step in and inspire your children to develop their God given potential.

The power of intuition, controlled by the right brain processor, is considered by the state system to be inferior brain power. Why? Because it is not evidence or logic based. Don't get me wrong. I agree with the use of left-brain processing, but I am saying it should not be at the gross neglect of right-brain processing.

There is something in the education system called peer review. This is a system whereby others review the validity of your research or opinion and validate its thesis based on the fact that your outcome is repeatable. There may be some merit to this, but not everything can be peer reviewed. When Daniel saw the vision he declared in Daniel 10:7 (ESV) that *"I alone saw the vision, for the men who were with me did not see the vision…"*

So how do you peer review Daniel's vision? Let's call a spade a spade. There are some things left brain cannot do.

Intuition is a function of the human spirit. It is the way God's Spirit speaks to the human spirit. Intuition is not based on subject-knowledge. Intuition enables the Holy Spirit speaks to the human spirit. So you can see why the devil wants to be sure the right brain processor is killed off. Once that is muted, it becomes difficult for you to relate with God in many respects.

Dominant left-brain usage can make believing difficult, as it seeks only logical and factual elements. This is the goal of the Amorite spirit that dominates the earth's educational system. Nearly everything Jesus did or said pulled on the right brain of human beings.

His principles were quite different from those of the Greek mentality that dominated the people at that time. So many of the things Jesus said frustrated the left-brain oriented people. His parables demanded picturing: *"The kingdom of God is like..."* Christ used many metaphors, pictures and stories, all right brain stuff.

Being able to understand what Jesus was saying requires you to suppress what you've been formally taught through the left brain because Jesus is always painting a picture, always trying to conceptualize something, which is not what left-brain dominated people do.

As we conclude this chapter, I will emphasise that the assignment of the Holy Spirit-gifted teacher is more profound than it appears. We can see now that it's not just about teaching people the basic curriculum of 1+1=2. It involves new curriculum and new methods of training, in ways that direct children to their God given destinies.

This is why we need to take over this mountain and to pray. We also need to be involved in education. Can you see the danger we are in right now?

The formal education system, being ruled by the Amorites, is structured to militate against everything God wants to do in our lives.

Therefore we need to reclaim this mountain. Otherwise our children will continue to be suppressed by the system. They will not come into the fullness of what God wants them to do, and then we will be perpetuating the processing plant of the enemy. He is churning out a generation of people who are led only by what they can see and not what they believe.

That is the mountain of education. Let me make it clear: left brain usage is necessary for learning, and I am not against that. All I am saying is that there is a need to develop the right-brain intuitive learning that we all have and make it a strong force that will moderate the rigidity of left-brain learning.

This will not happen unless believers get

involved in education at all three levels. There will also be need for more resources to be made available to education by those in government.

Can you see the foolishness of an introverted and isolated church posture? While all these things are happening in our world, in the media, in the government and in the schools, Christians are sitting down in a place called church, thinking it does not affect them and waiting for Jesus to return. What foolishness!

God is interested in having us disciple nations and that means reclaiming all these mountains for the Lord. When that happens, what the Bible says in the book of Revelation will become real: the kingdoms of this world will become the kingdoms of our God and of his Christ and he shall reign forever and ever. Hallelujah!

Note here your Key Learning Points from Chapter 9

CHAPTER 10

BREAKTHROUGH STRATEGIES IN THE <u>ECONOMY/BUSINESS</u> SECTOR

Mountain #4

In Deuteronomy the tribe that represents the mountain of business or economy are the Canaanites, and the significant ministry gift in the church that displaces them is prophetic grace.

I use the word *grace* rather than prophets, because you need not be a prophet to have influence. You need that grace. If I operate in prophetic grace on a particular day, that doesn't make me a prophet; it just means I'm operating in that grace for that period.

In Rev 5:12, the Lamb is proclaimed worthy to receive riches. This relates to that mountain.

When the Lord your God brings you into the land which you go to possess, and has cast out many nations before you, the Hittites and the Girgashites and the Amorites and the Canaanites.... seven nations greater and mightier than you... **Deuteronomy 7:1**

The economy is the system of *production, distribution* and *consumption* of resources. Any economy has these three elements, and it is healthy when there is a proper balance between them.

God help you if all you're doing is consuming. The truth is, that's what most poor people tend to do. They don't distribute and they don't produce.

A nation's legitimate economy can be divided into two broad groupings: the real economy and the financial economy. Every economic activity outside of the financial sector — manufacturing, distribution, haulage, etc. — I call the *real* economy.

In the real economy you are dealing with a tangible service or product, whereas in the financial economy you are dealing with funds and numbers. For those of you who doubt the power of the financial economy just look at what has happened in the world economy over the last few years. Notice how the same bankers who caused the financial collapse are now practically immune from further setbacks.

They are now paying themselves the same bonuses, even though they needed a bail-out from the public sector. We've seen from all the budget cuts announced by governments that the people who didn't cause the problem are now paying for its consequences.

The financial economy is that sector in which we can all participate, as our money can multiply 24 hours a day if we get our strategies right. As believers we are supposed to take part in both in the real economy and the financial economy. We cannot lay claim to prosperity if we don't.

The rulers over the mountain of economy are known as merchants or traffickers. The Promised Land was often called Canaan for short. That shows us its fruitfulness and abundance. Now, who is the king of the Canaanites who rules this mountain? You'll recognise his name. It is Mammon.

Mammon is a strong principality because it can totally impact the behaviour of its victims. Mammon's influence can lead to sexual immorality, addictions, corruption, pride, lust, and all manner of deviant behaviours. Mammon is strong because he harbours and facilitates all other sinful acts. That is why the Bible tells us we cannot serve two masters — God and Mammon. We have to love one and hate the other.

Mammon is the only demonic power that God knows can influence the entire life choices of human beings.

Mammon is also called Babylon in the book of Revelation. Mammon wrestles for God's seats in your life. Money is not something you gain because you are educated or qualified. *It is a spiritual force,* and until you understand this fully, you, as a child of God, must not rely on your qualifications alone to dabble in the marketplace. It will not work.

I have said money always flows in the direction of spiritual power. If you are to control riches of any tangible value on earth, you must possess spiritual power, either godly or demonic.

Satan, through Mammon, controls the economies of the world. We are either spiritually connected to him or we possess a superior spiritual power to dislodge him and reclaim his riches. So it is essentially a spiritual battle that we engage in.

Mammon tells you he is actually your source. Many buy into this deception, but once we do we are in deep trouble. We will begin to do everything contrary to the will of God, but Mammon will compensate us with money —at least for a season before destroying us.

The deception of the enemy must be discerned by those who are spiritually active. Mammon's influence shows up in an excessive desire for money and wealth, otherwise known as *greed*.

When greed takes hold of us we become unreasonable and unrestrained in our quest for money. Mammon, unlike some of the other principalities, seeks to control *all* areas of our life once we are under its control. That is why those who have been given money by Mammon subsequently commit all manner of abuses.

The Canaanite spirit (Mammon) has two goals:
1. To oppose God by putting people under the stress of wanting more and more without ever being content. The first shot Mammon gives you is insatiable greed. You become impossible to satisfy.
2. To put people under pressures which seem to threaten their survival.

We will find ourselves in circumstances so dire that our very survival seems imperilled. What we do not understand is that we are close to our breakthrough.

The enemy has a way of making things worse than they are, but the darkest part of the night is just before the dawn. So we must not give up while we are in the process.

If we are contending daily with how to put bread on the table, preaching the gospel is the last thing on our mind, so poverty is an enemy tactic that needs to be dealt with.

We cannot capture this mountain if we are under the spirit that rules it. So we cannot take the mountain of economy/business if we are under the influence of Mammon. We must be delivered first. And for that to happen, we must go through God's process and brokenness.

We must go through the threshing floor where God will get out of us anything that Mammon could use to control us with. God will deal with our pride. He will deal with our ego. He will deal with our reputation. He will empty us out before he then fills us afresh. Process is painful.

We lose our pride and our ego is battered. Any of things the enemy can use — things like pride, personal ambition, inordinate ambition — all are gotten rid of in such a way that when Mammon comes near us he can't function because we are already emptied of those things he could use.

We cannot dominate a mountain if we are already a slave to its predominant spirit. Jesus showed how to have victory over Mammon when it was said *the enemy came and found nothing in him* (John 14:30). It means Mammon was looking for something to hold onto in Jesus but could find nothing.

We must cleanse ourselves from the love of money, and the strongest way to do this is through giving. Many of the richest people in the world today are also big givers.

God brings wealth and we give. Then we believe God into thousands, into hundreds of thousands, and gradually into millions. But some of us give peanuts and expect an elephant-sized harvest. It doesn't work that way.

We need to cleanse ourselves from the love of money, because those who take over the mountain of business are the ones that control the financial resources of nations, and that won't happen if we are slaves of greed and Mammon.

But God said to him, "Fool! This night your soul will be required of you; then whose will those things be which you have provided?" [21] *So is he who lays up treasure for himself, and is not rich toward God."* **Luke 12:20-21**

But those who desire to be rich fall into temptation and a snare, and into many foolish and harmful lusts which drown men in destruction and perdition. [10] *For the love of money is a root of all kinds of evil, for which some have strayed from the faith in their greediness, and pierced themselves through with many sorrows.* **1 Timothy 6:9-10**

This scripture is unequivocal. You will fall into temptation if you desire to be rich. Not maybe or sometime. It is guaranteed. Yet how many people will say they don't want to be rich?

This scripture explains why a desire to be rich and the accompanying greed has led many astray, into falsehood and unspeakable acts of iniquity.

Agur displayed unparalleled wisdom in his unique prayer in the book of Proverbs.

[7]Two things I request of you (deprive me not before I die): [8] *Remove falsehood and lies far from me; Give me neither poverty nor riches.*

Feed me with the food allotted to me, ⁹ lest I be full and deny you, and say, "Who is the Lord?" Or lest I be poor and steal, and profane the name of my God. **Proverbs 30:7-9**

How many of us can pray that? Yes, we all can pray that God not give us poverty, but how many can pray that God not give them riches? This reveals the problem with this generation. Agur prayed that God should give him sufficient food. This is a wise attitude.

What does it mean to "desire to be rich?" To understand this phrase we have to look at what other Bible translations of 1 Timothy 6:9 say on this matter.

They that will be rich fall into temptation and a snare... (KJV)

People who want to get rich fall into temptation and a trap..... (NIV)

Those who crave to be rich fall into temptation and a snare...(Amp.)

People who long to be rich fall into temptation and are trapped by many foolish and harmful desires...... (NLT)

Those who buy into Christianity to serve their

turn for this world will be disappointed, but those who embrace it as their lifestyle will find it has the promise of abundant life now as well as in the world to come.

When reduced to the most straightened circumstances, we cannot be poorer than when we came into this world. A shroud, a coffin, and a grave are all that the richest people can have from all their wealth.

The necessities of life bound the desires of true Christians, and with these we will endeavour to be content. We see here the evil of covetousness. It is not said they that are rich, but that they will be rich, who place their happiness in wealth, and are determined in its pursuit.

Such people give to Satan the opportunity of tempting them, leading them to use dishonest means, and other bad practices to add to their gains. Beware of striving for riches at all costs. A zeal for earthly wealth will lead to greed-led living.

Therefore the phrase *desire to be rich* refers to the focused pursuit of wealth without an understanding of God's purpose for it. The desires of humankind are acceptable to God only if they fulfill his purpose and advance his kingdom.

So what is God's purpose for wealth? If you cannot answer this question correctly then your desire to be rich is not rooted in God and will lead to your downfall. As I will explain in the coming chapters, is it not curious that God gave all the processed gold and silver of Egypt to the children of Israel, and yet he led them through the wilderness for the next forty years where there was no shop to spend it!

For those forty years the people were fed by manna from heaven. Water came out of the rock for them, and their shoes and clothes did not wear out. In short, they were miraculously sustained even though their pockets were full of gold. Clearly, if God is not your sustainer no amount of money can sustain you.

If God is not your source then you are a poor indeed.

Ten dangers of desiring to be rich without knowing God's purpose for wealth (from 1 Tim 6:9-10)
a) You will fall into the temptations of the devil.
b) You will fall into the traps of the devil.
c) You will be at the mercy of foolish lusts.
d) You will be at the mercy of hurtful lusts.

e) Destruction and perdition await you.
f) The root of evil will grow in you.
g) You will stray from the faith.
h) Many sorrows will befall you.
i) High-mindedness and pride will come upon you
j) You will invest your trust in wrong things and people

In all of this God is saying we should not pursue money. We don't have what it takes. Mammon will kill all who are greedy for gain.

What causes a person to pursue wealth for the wrong reasons?
This is the big question. To understand what led to this temptation, we must go back to the Garden of Eden. We need to ask, what made Eve fall for the serpent in the first place? How did the serpent succeed in deceiving her? Clearly she was not entrapped by the things that bedevil our modern society.

- She was not entrapped by riches; because she owned everything in the Garden.
- She was not entrapped by sexual immorality or lust, because Adam was the only man around.
- She was not entrapped by jealousy, because there was no other woman in the

garden.

Eve was in a perfect environment, and yet she fell for the trap of *dissatisfaction.*

Dissatisfaction made her forget the hundreds of other trees and focus on just one, to her detriment. Others today will do likewise, turning their backs on thousands of blessings to foolishly pursue one item to their destruction.

And it is, indeed, a source of immense profit, for godliness accompanied with contentment (that contentment which is a sense of inward sufficiency) is great and abundant gain. **1 Timothy 6:6 (AMP)**

Dissatisfaction is the mother of greed. Eve could be tempted only because she had lost her sense of satisfaction. She was infected with discontent.

Hell and Destruction] are never full; so the eyes of man are never satisfied. **Proverbs 27:20**

The only dissatisfaction God allows is dissatisfaction with sin and mediocrity. Materially, we must learn contentment. Money boasts of what it cannot deliver. It can buy medicine but not health. Money can buy a house, but not a home. God wants us blessed more than we can imagine, but he knows our hearts need to be right.

Oh, satisfy us early with your mercy, that we may rejoice and be glad all our days! **Psalm 90:14**

Dissatisfaction will prevent us from understanding God's purpose. Let us embrace godly satisfaction and stop comparing ourselves with others.

How precious is your steadfast love, O God! The children of men take refuge and put their trust under the shadow of your wings. They relish and feast on the abundance of your house; and you cause them to drink of the stream of your pleasures. For with you is the fountain of life; in your light do we see light. - **Psalm 36:7-9**

The process of becoming
When we are living in contentment, there is one more thing God will do before he will invest us with his abundant wealth and the strategy to reclaim this mountain. God will take us through *process*.

It is during this time that God empties us of anything that mammon can use to gain a foothold in our lives. The Bible reveals that even Jesus was emptied.

I will not talk with you much more, for the prince (evil genius, ruler) of the world is coming. And he has no claim on me. [He has nothing in common with me; **there is nothing in me that belongs to him,** *and he has no power over me.]* **John 14:30 (Amp.)**

Jesus said there was nothing in him that belonged to the devil. Can we say the same thing? This is why God will take us through process and brokenness. Through it we will learn to imbibe certain key values and virtues.

¹¹ But you, man of God, flee from all this, and pursue righteousness, godliness, faith, love, endurance and gentleness. ¹² Fight the good fight of the faith. Take hold of the eternal life to which you were called when you made your good confession in the presence of many witnesses. ¹³ In the sight of God, who gives life to everything, and of Christ Jesus, who while testifying before Pontius Pilate made the good confession, I charge you ¹⁴ to keep this command without spot or blame until the appearing of our Lord Jesus Christ, ¹⁵ which God will bring about in his own time – God, the blessed and only Ruler, the King of kings and Lord of lords, ¹⁶ who alone is immortal and who lives in unapproachable light, whom no one has seen or can see. To him be honour and might for ever. Amen.

¹⁷ Command those who are rich in this present world not to be arrogant nor to put their hope in wealth, which is so uncertain, but to put their hope in God, who richly provides us with everything for our enjoyment. ¹⁸ Command them to do good, to be rich in good deeds, and to be generous and willing to share. **1 Timothy 6:11-18**

Eight things we learn during process
1. We learn how not to be high-minded or proud. God will take us through the threshing floor of shame and pain to empty us of our pride and ego so that he can fill us afresh.
2. We learn not to trust in uncertain riches. By making sure we lack them, God will show us the deceitfulness and uncertain nature of Mammon, so that we learn not to trust in it for the rest of our lives.
3. We will learn to trust in the living God only. We will come out of process trusting God alone, as everything else will have failed us.
4. We will learn to do good, that is, to gain character.
5. We will learn to be rich in good works.
6. We will come out ready and willing to distribute. Nobody who has been through process will need to be begged to give. It will become a lifestyle.

7. We will lay up treasures in heaven, where it matters. We will become more Kingdom minded.
8. We will lay hold of eternal life.

It is only after process that God can begin to invest us with his true riches. The spirit of dissatisfaction is married to the spirit of Mammon. Pray against the spirit of dissatisfaction. Let us ask God to reveal to us what our portion is.

As it is written: "What no eye has seen, what no ear has heard, and what no human mind has conceived the things God has prepared for those who love him" – these are the things God has revealed to us by his Spirit. The Spirit searches all things, even the deep things of God. For who knows a person's thoughts except their own spirit within them? In the same way no one knows the thoughts of God except the Spirit of God. What we have received is not the spirit of the world, but the Spirit who is from God, so that we may understand what God has freely given us. **1 Corinthians 2:9-12 (NIV)**

Keep your lives free from the love of money and be content with what you have, because God has said, "Never will I leave you; never will I forsake you. So we say with confidence, "The Lord is my helper; I will not be afraid. What can mere mortals do to me?" **Hebrews 13:5-6 (NIV)**

Let your investment be in heaven, and may you lean contentment in Jesus' name.

The purpose of the Christian take-over and reclamation this mountain is to facilitate the end-time wealth transfer as predicted in the Scriptures. It is about dislodging Satan from his last domain of occupation, and the fight will be bloody. He will throw everything he has at you.

That is why in preparing you for the fight, God takes you through process. He empties you of any love of money. He embeds in you an understanding of his divine purpose for wealth. Then you are ready to reclaim this mountain.

A good man leaves an inheritance [of moral stability and goodness] to his children's children, and the wealth of the sinner [finds its way eventually] into the hands of the righteous, for whom it was laid up. **Proverbs 13:22 (AMP)**

God's end-time prophetic agenda
*For, behold, **the darkness** shall cover the earth, and gross darkness the people: but the Lord shall arise upon thee, and his glory shall be seen upon thee.* **Isaiah 60:2**

God's Word says *the darkness* shall cover the

earth. The use of the definite article *"the"* signifies a darkness that has been programmed to cover the earth. It has been determined, and it will not be partial but total. There will be an absence of light for the people of the world.

The things that will happen will defy every known solution. People will run from pillar to post, but all in vain, as answers elude them. The only light that will be seen shining mysteriously from above. This is the light of God's glory which he will release upon his people alone!

This is God's prophetic agenda. Every time God wants to humble a people, one of the things he uses is hunger.

And he humbled thee, and suffered thee to hunger... **Deuteronomy 8:3**

He humbled them with hunger, thirst and nakedness. It is easier to get at a man if food is used as a weapon. God is going to humble this generation! There is going to be a wave of financial hardship which has been gathering momentum for the past few years. Many are already its victims. God has said this earth will burn like an oven. The reason is just to humble the proud.

God is targeting the proud so he can humble

them. The time has come to humiliate them, while the time of manifestation has come for the saints. The time has come for all who do wickedly to know that God is the Governor among nations. Everyone you see today who is not a Christian has a bleak future, no matter what they have gathered. Their wealth will all be transferred to the just. To reclaim this mountain is not only doable — it is predicted and certain. So be encouraged, folks.

To reclaim the mountain of economy/business we need Christians who have been pruned and fashioned in the temple before being sent into the marketplace. We need believers who have a good grasp of Scripture and of God's purpose for wealth.

More importantly, we need believers who are entrepreneurial and business minded, believers who are not just satisfied with working for others and collecting a salary, but interested in employing others. Christians who are employees need divine insight into how to get to the top in their various organisations.

We must also be prepared. Concerning Jotham, the Bible says in 2 Chronicles 27:6: *Jotham became mighty, because he prepared his ways before the Lord his God.*

Greatness is prepared for. It is not jumped into or stumbled upon. Nobody succeeds by accident. Every great sportsperson has made preparations to attain their greatness.

Let us labour for the Word of God to be effectual in our lives. We must give what it takes to stand on the Word, by the Word and for the Word. It is time to exercise ourselves unto the covenant of God, to bring out the star in us.

A few years ago I wrote a book titled *Secrets of Biblical Wealth Transfer*. I suggest you get it as goes into more detail on how this transfer will take place.

To reclaim this mountain we also need the force of righteousness. We need to be strengthened within by God's Spirit, so we will be able to say no to what looks good; because we understand that *there is a way that appears to be right, but in the end it leads to death.* **Proverbs 14:12 (NIV)**

We must choose not to walk in deception. You cannot take a mountain from a spirit whose influence you are under. Referring to Babylon in Revelation 18:2-3, the Bible says:

Fallen! Fallen is Babylon the Great! She has become a dwelling for demons and a haunt for every impure spirit, a haunt for every unclean bird, a haunt for every unclean and detestable animal. For all the nations have drunk the maddening wine of her adulteries. The kings of the earth committed adultery with her, and the merchants of the earth grew rich from her excessive luxuries. Rev. 18:2-3

You can see that Mammon of Babylon has a way of supplying his own people. They become rich through his activities, remember the devil fattens the cow before he kills it. So do not be deceived.

Revelation 18 warns believers of a time when the economic system of this world will collapse. Wealth itself will not collapse, but the present system of trade will seize, as it were.

In Revelation 18:4-6 we read:
Then I heard another voice from heaven say:
"'Come out of her, my people, so that you will not share in her sins, so that you will not receive any of her plagues. For her sins are piled up to heaven, and God has remembered her crimes. Give back to her as she has given; pay her back double for what she has done. Pour her a double portion from her own cup."

You can see that God is, metaphorically, asking us to come out of the Babylonian system. This means we need to create (as we enter the mountain of economy) and to establish new patterns of doing things.

God's call for his people is to extricate ourselves from being under this principality and the system it has created. In order to take this mountain we will need to reject the thought patterns and behaviours of Babylon, in terms of the way it thinks and behaves. We'll need to live independently of the system of this world.

Personal reclamation strategies
How do you begin to reclaim this mountain?
1. Initiate a strategy that will involve *active prayer* for this mountain. Begin to pray for the mountain of economy of the nation.
2. Prayerfully *determine if you have been personally called* to this mountain. Ask God: Is this the predominant mountain I have been called to reclaim for you? Having a job does not mean you have been called to the mountain. Most people who work at present do so out of the need to put food on the table. That is different from being called to reclaim this mountain.
3. Discover the God-given dominant gift that you will use to explore this mountain.
God has given each of us a personal gifting to impact this mountain, but what is your gifting? In other words, what gift has God given you to be

able to dominate the mountain of economy?

In 1 Corinthians 12:12-18 we read:
¹² Just as a body, though one, has many parts, but all its many parts form one body, so it is with Christ. ¹³ For we were all baptised by one Spirit so as to form one body – whether Jews or Gentiles, slave or free – and we were all given the one Spirit to drink. ¹⁴ And so the body is not made up of one part but of many.
¹⁵ Now if the foot should say, 'Because I am not a hand, I do not belong to the body,' it would not for that reason stop being part of the body. ¹⁶ And if the ear should say, 'Because I am not an eye, I do not belong to the body,' it would not for that reason stop being part of the body. ¹⁷ If the whole body were an eye, where would the sense of hearing be? If the whole body were an ear, where would the sense of smell be? ¹⁸ But in fact God has placed the parts in the body, every one of them, just as he wanted them to be.

Psalm 115:1-7 also refers to the body, but talks about idols:
Not to us, Lord, not to us but to your name be the glory, because of your love and faithfulness.
² Why do the nations say 'Where is their God?'
³ Our God is in heaven; he does whatever pleases him. ⁴ But their idols are silver and gold, made by human hands. ⁵ They have mouths,

but cannot speak, eyes, but cannot see. ⁶ They have ears, but cannot hear, noses, but cannot smell.⁷ They have hands, but cannot feel, feet, but cannot walk, nor can they utter a sound with their throats.

Until we get rid of the idols in our lives, our talents (gifts) cannot come alive. Anything we have elevated above God in our life is an idol. It can be money, assets, career, spouse or even our ministry.

These two scriptures show we have been given seven categories of Christian giftings to use, to reclaim the marketplace. In other words, every believer on the face of the earth has one of these as a dominant gifting, and it has nothing to do with our training. I'm talking of what we were born to do. We may be an eye type, a nose type, a feet type, a hand type, an ear type, a mouth type or a head type.

Which type are you?
Matthew 25:14-30 - ¹⁴ *"For the kingdom of heaven is like a man travelling to a far country, who called his own servants and delivered his goods to them. ¹⁵And to one he gave five talents, to another two, and to another one,* **to each according to his own ability**; *and immediately he went on a journey. ¹⁶Then he who had received the five talents went and*

traded with them, and made another five talents. ¹⁷And likewise he who had received two gained two more also. ¹⁸But he who had received one went and dug in the ground, and hid his lord's money. ¹⁹After a long time the lord of those servants came and settled accounts with them. ²⁰"So he who had received five talents came and brought five other talents, saying, "Lord, you delivered to me five talents; look, I have gained five more talents besides them.' ²¹His lord said to him, "Well done, good and faithful servant; you were faithful over a few things, I will make you ruler over many things. Enter into the joy of your lord.' ......
*²⁴"Then he who had received the one talent came and said, "Lord, I knew you to be a hard man, reaping where you have not sown, and gathering where you have not scattered seed. ²⁵And I was afraid, and went and hid your talent in the ground. Look, there you have what is yours.' ²⁶"But his lord answered and said to him, "You wicked and lazy servant, you knew that I reap where I have not sown, and gather where I have not scattered seed. ²⁷So you ought to have deposited my money with the bankers, and at my coming I would have received back my own with interest. ²⁸So take the talent from him, and give it to him who has ten talents. ²⁹"**For to everyone who has, more will be given,** and he will have abundance; but from him who does not have, even what he has will be taken away.*

³⁰*And cast the unprofitable servant into the outer darkness. There will be weeping and gnashing of teeth.'*

To reclaim this mountain, God has given all of us talents. But why, like this wicked servant, are some people not able to produce a result?

- Each time there is an inability to produce in your life, it is because you have not identified, or invested, your God-given talents.
- Each time there is an inability to produce in your life, it is because you have invested your time in areas where you have no talents.

So we need to know what our ability is and how we can use it to reclaim the mountain of business. Everything we need has already been given to us by God. All we need do is produce and increase.

I can do all things through Christ who strengthens me, but God's strength is available only in the area of our God-given talents and abilities.

THE SEVEN TALENT GROUPS

Seven categories of Christian talents / enterprise that are needed to reclaim the mountain of business

Based on the parts of the body we identified in 1 Corinthians 12:12-18, we can see what is needed to reclaim this mountain.

Foot cannot do the work of hand. Eyes cannot do the work of eye. But which part are you? There are seven types of giftedness/talents in the kingdom of God. We need to locate our dominant gifting before we can accurately reclaim this sector of the Marketplace.

Talent 1: THE HAND GROUP

These are *artisans, handcrafters, sculptors, painters, hairdressers and artists.* They can create anything with their hands. Many of them are artisans in the Bible. Hand people may not necessarily be academically brilliant.

They make money from the creativity of their hands.

1 Corinthians 4 - *[12]And we labour, working with our own hands. Being reviled, we bless; being persecuted, we endure; [13]being defamed, we entreat. We have been made as the filth of the world, …until now.*

Talent 2: THE FEET GROUP

The feet people are usually *pioneers and innovators*. They are foot soldiers. They cannot stay at home. They cannot stay behind a desk. If they do they will become frustrated. They are mobile, outdoor people. If you are the foot type, stop wasting your time applying for jobs you can't get.

Why have you stayed unemployed for months and years, believing God, when you could have been making money using your hands? If we were all office managers, who would fix your drains? Stay in the area of your giftedness.

Talent 3: THE EAR GROUP

These are the speculators. They pick up things from God's transmitter. They are investors, brokers, stock market workers. They are prophetic in their hearing.

They usually have their ears to the ground. They know what is going to move before anyone else does. They could hear money making tips from what others ignore.

Talent 4: THE EYE GROUP

The eye people are the visionaries. They make something out of nothing. They are dreamers. Their strength is in their ability to foresee things and capitalize on this. They are leaders who inspire others. Like Bill gates, they make money out of motivating others in a set direction. They see potential where others see junk.

Talent 5: THE NOSE GROUP
These are the wheeler dealers. They have connections in high places. These types of people have lots of unbeliever connections. God can use them to take wealth from sinners. They can smell a deal a mile off. They have brief cases, but sometime no office. They get contracts, they subcontract to the experts, and they pocket the profit.

The first chunk of money I made as a business person was in 1989. All I did was to get a contract from an oil company through a contact. Then I subcontracted it to a local team and pocketed the difference. So what can you smell?

Talent 6: THE MOUTH GROUP
These are the motivational speakers, or orators. They are commentators, and sales people. They are newscasters. They are preachers and teachers. They are lawyers and advocates. These people do a lot of research to get their facts right. Then they deliver the message with authority.

By the way, if you are the mouth type, you must

take care of your mouth. A smelly mouth is a weapon of mass destruction.

Talent 7: THE HEAD TYPE
These are the thinkers. They may be the invisible hand behind major enterprise breakthrough. Many of them are laboratory animals. They don't like confronting customers. They like the back office.

They are champions of the knowledge economy. Many of them are professors. Are you inclined that way? Then you need to begin to use that gift to promote righteousness in the marketplace.

Why has God given us these seven gifting? Your ability to dominate or reclaim the mountain of economy is linked to whether you are using your dominant gifting group.

Remember, the grace of God dwells in your life maximally if you are working in your area of expertise. If you are moving away from that centre, you are moving towards your vulnerability. So if you are not using your primary gifting, it's difficult for you to succeed in the market place.

Find out which gift you have, because you are going to confront many enemies in the market place and doing what you are born to do makes it easy to win over the enemy. You'll enjoy your work even as you confront discouragement and attack from all the marketplace demons. If you are doing what you were born to do it's easy to motivate yourself, whereas if you are doing it simply because you want to put bread on the table, it's easy to be discouraged from it.

You cannot take over the market place if you are not using your dominant gifting. In Luke 19:13, the master called ten of his servants, delivered to them ten minas and told them, "Do business until I come. Occupy till I come, engage in business until I come. Put this money to use until I return."

We are supposed to be doing business until the Lord returns. We need to unlock divine provision that eliminates financial hardship. Let's discover our talent and do business with it until he comes. Hallelujah!

The Final Frontier

After Paul's dramatic conversion, he spent fourteen years in Damascus, being taught by the Holy Spirit. He explained to the church at Ephesus:

For this reason I, Paul, the prisoner of Christ Jesus for the sake of you Gentiles –

² Surely you have heard about the administration of God's grace that was given to me for you, ³ that is, the mystery made known to me by revelation, as I have already written briefly. ⁴ In reading this, then, you will be able to understand my insight into the mystery of Christ, ⁵ which was not made known to people in other generations as it has now been revealed by the Spirit to God's holy apostles and prophets. **–Ephesians 3:3-5, NIV.**

From this scripture we see that God often reveals the "big picture" to his apostles. In Paul's generation it was the mystery of the Gentiles being included in God's plan of the ages.

Paul's generation saw the transition from the age of Law to the age of Grace. In our generation, the Lord is revealing the transition from the age of Grace to the age of the Kingdom, which includes the marriage of the Lamb to his bride-body church.

This larger vision is often what distinguishes apostles. So there will be many marketplace apostles raised up in this age of the Kingdom. They will participate in, and disciple other Christians in, the demon-infested world of business and wealth creation.

Ron McKenzie writes in his excellent book *Being Church Where We Live*:

"*A church with an apostolic vision will train people up and send them out to work in the business world. The Kingdom of God expands as Christians extend the rule of God into areas of life where they have authority. Authority is an essential aspect of any kingdom. This means Christians should seek positions of authority to help God's Kingdom to expand.*"

This outcome is the purpose of this book on the reclamation of the marketplace.

Note here your Key Learning Points from Chapter 10

CHAPTER 11

BREAKTHROUGH STRATEGIES IN <u>ARTS, ENTERTAINMENT, MOVIES, FASHION</u> AND RELATED SECTORS

Mountain #5

I have repeatedly used the word *reclaim* when dealing with the marketplace. To *reclaim* means to get back what used to be ours, because the Bible says "The earth is the Lord's and the fullness thereof." It's not about trying to get it for the first time. We had it, but we lost it at Eden.

All that God did was for the benefit and enjoyment of his people, not for Satan. The Promised Land is our destination. And we know that "the kingdoms of this world will become the kingdoms of our God and of his Christ." The Bible also makes it clear that when the children of Israel were about to go into the land, God specifically told them that before they could possess it, they needed to conquer seven enemies, seven spirits, seven nations.

The seven nations were greater and mightier than Israel, and, as we have seen so far, they represented satanic barriers to getting to the Promised Land.

"When the Lord your God brings you into the land you are entering to possess and drives out before you many nations – the Hittites, Girgashites, Amorites, Canaanites, Perizzites, **Hivites** *... seven nations larger and stronger than you* **Deut.7:1**

Now the tribe in Deuteronomy that represents dominance in the sphere of entertainment, arts, movies and fashion are the **Hivites**.

In 1998, in the USA, a survey was done using the question, *Do you believe in God?* In the general population, 93 per cent said they believed in God. In the military it was 90 per cent, in the business community it was 70 per cent, and among politicians 50 per cent.

But in the sector of arts, fashion and entertainment, the percentage of believers dropped to 3 per cent.

It is this influential and the entirely godless sector that is moulding and influencing trends in our nations. And sadly, for a long time Christians abandoned that mountain almost entirely.

It used to be considered a sin for believers to be involved in the world of fashion design. In the 1970s and 1980s, for example, in many part of Africa mega churches emerged that spoke against dressing well, and wearing jewellery. They even spoke against the use of perfumes.

So working in this sector was almost certainly taboo to many Christians. What foolishness! Lots of people in church, even today, still think it is the devil's area. *Just leave it and don't go there.* As a result of this historical mindset, Satan has populated this sector with his own people, almost without opposition. Yet we are all affected by it now.

International news services reported that after Afghanistan was invaded by coalition forces in search of Osama bin Laden, the first public buildings in Afghanistan to re-open were not hospitals, schools or government agencies.

Instead, in this strongly Muslim country, they were movie theatres, showing American films. This shows how the arts culture influences a whole generation. Some more examples follow. In 1934, in the movie *It Happened One Night*, the popular star Clark Gable performed without an undershirt to better display his physique. Thereafter it was reported that undershirt sales dropped dramatically in the USA.

In 1942, when the movie *Bambi* premiered, deer hunting in America dropped from a 5.7 million dollar business to one of less than a million. Why? Because the little deer suddenly became something people wanted to hug more than to shoot. The point I am making is that what people see in the movies influences their lives in a real way.

It is the job of art and entertainment to create an imaginary world and use it to shape popular culture and fashion trends. This is one sector Christians should never have abandoned. But because we've left it completely in the hands of the enemy, it now influences an entire generation — one in which the Church is not yet making enough impact. The mountain of arts and entertainment creates sounds and sights that promote Satan's control of popular culture. Such sounds and sights are irresistible.

Who is the ruler of this mountain?
The Hivite spirit rules this mountain. And the commanding principality on this mountain of arts

and entertainment is a demon called **Jezebel**. I'm sure many of you have heard the name. The name means *unchaste or "Baal is my husband."* She is always leading people astray. We must constantly be on guard against her allurement. Otherwise we'll find ourselves living counterfeit lives of deception and perversion.

Jezebel is associated with *lust and seduction*. Seduction is perversely misrepresented as romance and lust is masked as love. If you think of the things Jezebel leads people to do in name of sexual liberty, you will be shocked.

Hivites are also the enemy villagers who are occupying the life-giving place. They represent counterfeit and perversion. They are experts at misrepresenting reality. Does that begin to sound like the movies to you? One of the key things the Hivites are known for in Scripture is their sexual perversion. The first mention of the Hivites is in Genesis 34, where we find a Hivite raping a girl.

There is always a sexually perverted element to the Hivites and you see this in the arts and entertainment industry. That's what they do.

I have never understood, for example, why a half-naked woman is used to sell a car. Does that have anything to do with the wheels or steering? There is no correlation. What the advertisers are doing is using imagery to appeal to your sexual weaknesses. Then you assume that if you drive that car, girls of that nature will be attracted to you. Many people are buying the lies. Why else would the industry be growing year in and year in the way it does?

The Hivites show up again in Joshua 9:3. The Gibeonites were Hivites and they caused Joshua to make a treaty not to kill them by pretending to be people they were not. So we see the Hivites were manipulative. Later, in Joshua 9:22, Joshua accused the Gibeonites of having "beguiled" him. The word in Hebrew is *rama* which means to deceive or mislead.

Those are the objectives of the current global arts and entertainment sector. You should view this sector with a healthy scepticism from now on. It is particularly important when we are talking about the music industry.

There are two categories of angels in heaven; the normal angels and the archangels. The archangels are few in number.

The psalmist says (Psalm 8:4-5):
What is mankind that you are mindful of them, human beings that you care for them? You have made them a little lower than the

angels and crowned them with glory and honour.

In other words the hierarchy after creation was God (top), then Adam, then archangels, then normal angels. This is partly what led to the pride and jealousy of Lucifer — seeing man above him in status. Before Lucifer fell, he was the chief musician in heaven.

Anything creative in heaven, he was in charge of. He was the one to do the design of the angelic clothing, he led the angels who played in the orchestra, and he composed the music. It made him very talented in this area.

Understand that when Lucifer fell, even though he was sent out of heaven he was not deprived of his powers, because the Bible in Romans 11:29 that the gifts and calling of God are irrevocable.

So when Lucifer fell, along with a third of the angels in heaven, he fell with all his powers intact. He then tricked his way into getting the title deed to the earth. We have seen that his whole manipulation in the garden was not targeted at Adam per se.

He was interested in a territory where he could have influence and operate legally. And he has put his musical and creative talents to good use here, to perpetuate his hold on the earth through this mountain.

The mountain includes art, music, fashion, sports, movies, entertainment and anything we celebrate. It has been so captured by Satan that many saints do not believe it can be won back. I've met people who said the enemy had gone so far down this road that they wondered where a reclamation could start from. It is through this mountain that creativity shows up.

This mountain can and must be reclaimed for God, however, because it has captured the hearts of our youth the most. Anywhere you go in the nations, you see that the way many youth dress is informed by all the outputs of this mountain. The fan worship of celebrities has made the influence seem even greater, as many change their appearance to reflect the latest fad.

Many children today will not wear anything unless it has a designer label on it. But being cool should be less about what the next celebrity is wearing tomorrow, and more about what they are comfortable in.

Fashions come and go, and come back again. The question is, who determines what is cool?

For several years of their lives this sector is the only mountain that many of the youth care about. This mountain is what influences them the most, and the enemy has captured and thwarted the destiny of an entire generation.

Allow me to illustrate some more. If you were a footballer and were sent to prison for whatever reason, you would most likely be the football coach in prison, wouldn't you? If you were a musician and were sent to prison, you would most likely be the entertainer in prison because people naturally play to their strength in any environment.

This is exactly what Lucifer did. As heaven's chief musician, he was in charge of anything celebratory and creative. When he fell, he started using those giftings and powers to further his agenda on earth.

Did you know that music can create mood? You can listen to certain music and be happy and to certain other music and almost be crying because it of the bad memories it elicits. That is why some songs are easier to sing at funerals than at weddings. It's all about creating moods.

I tell young children not to get involved with worldly music because when they do they are not only buying into the music but also into the influence behind the music. When you understand that the person who orchestrates the whole thing is Satan himself, you have to ask yourself, *what benefit will it be for me?* These days when you talk to Christian children, they can name a hundred unbelieving artists before they can name five gospel artists. Why is this?

I realised long ago that you can't completely ban MTV and similar platforms because there is a need to know that this music exists, and our children do not live in isolation from others. But it is better to develop their spiritual capacity to see beyond it.

We need to remember that all these things are seeking to influence us and our children and to create a mood. What moods are we creating with the music we listen to? Some of the lyrics of these songs induce people to confess bad things over themselves, and Satan puts his stamp on this.

For example, when we have a song that says *I'm sad and depressed,* and we spend our day humming it, how are we going to be happy? It is important not to get ourselves things that will create negative emotions and make it hard for us to serve God.

Parents must do the best they can to train their children aright and ensure they understand the impact of these things. There's no way we can play praise and worship for a week without our spiritual life being changed that week.

Our countenance will change, our mood will change, and our love for God will increase. Conversely, we can be sad in the midst of happiness because of the music we listen to. Let us feed on things that will encourage and promote our walk with God.

In Old Testament times, sometimes when kings and prophets wanted to hear from God they would ask for a minstrel to play music first. Afterwards they were able to say, "Thus saith the Lord."

I read an article some time ago about how evil is developing at a fast pace in our generation, and that people are creating all manner of evil almost on a daily basis. Sometimes some people wake up and say, what evil can I perpetrate today? The interesting thing about these evils is that they are often protected by human rights and equality laws.

If we don't do anything about this mountain, within twenty years godliness and virtue will become non-existent.

Music and fashion trends have created many sub-cultures that influence people without their understanding the satanic impact. My challenge to you as you read this book is to develop the spiritual sensitivity to see Satan's grand plan to keep his dominance in the marketplace. He uses the creative sector to create images and sounds that control the actions of many.

Particularly in the Western world, Christians are failing to see the demons around them in Armani and other designer suits. The representation of the devil as a dark, creepy character with horns is a deliberate creation of Satan to prevent people from recognising his true identity and nature.

Evil is not easily seen through external appearances. You need spiritual insight to see that a person who looks well dressed and official can still be an agent of Satan. Do not be deceived, folks. Evil is around us daily. So never let your guard down, for your and for your children's sake.

How do we reclaim this mountain?
Jezebel is associated with lust and seduction. There are genuine pleasures in God, but Jezebel perverts everything. Psalm 16:11 says, *"You make known to me the path of life; you will fill me with joy in your presence, with eternal*

pleasures at your right hand." So pleasures are not an exclusive preserve of the devil. We need believers to begin to penetrate this industry and set the right standards one by one.

We are going to take over the movie studios one by one, and the fashion houses one by one, and to set standards. But believers have to be equipped and ready to do the work. This requires believers who have an affinity for arts, fashion, music, sports, movies and so on to understand that they are not there just to join the flock and become like the rest.

They are there as ambassadors of Christ, dropped behind enemy lines to penetrate the deep belly of Babylon in order to impact it for God. We need, in our generation, people who see themselves as God's CIA or FBI agents within those industries, people who will use the inspiration God is giving them to turn things around rather than just blend in and carry out business as usual.

At God's right hand are pleasures for evermore, but Jezebel seeks to entice us to be lovers of pleasure more than lovers of God.

"People will be lovers of themselves, lovers of money, boastful, proud, abusive, disobedient to their parents, ungrateful, unholy, [3] *without love,*

unforgiving, slanderous, without self-control, brutal, not lovers of the good, ⁴ treacherous, rash, conceited, lovers of pleasure rather than lovers of God – ⁵ *having a form of godliness but denying its power. Have nothing to do with such people".* **2 Timothy 3:2-5 (NIV).**

Avoid temptation
I read some time ago about a group of single Christian men who decided they would never look lustfully at women, and they prided themselves on their hundred per cent success rate so far.

As part of this experiment, they stayed in a house, from morning till evening and the only kind of music playing was love music —Marvin Gaye's *Sexual Healing* and the like — throughout the day. The second day repeated the exercise, but by the third day when they did a survey of these same people, 70 percent of them had changed.

After hearing words like "I want to hold you, I want to touch you," one's God-given imagination seeks something to hold. I use this illustration to show that songs which don't necessarily have bad words (like die or kill) can be equally dangerous in some circumstances.

These kinds of songs have a message, and

unless you have a place where you can channel it, trouble and sin can follow. If you are married and you listen to that message and you feel like holding your wife or husband, that song might be safe for you. But if you are not married and you keep listening to songs like that, then who are you going to hold?

So don't even go there. The Bible says, *Can you hold fire in your bosom and not get burned?* Jezebel is good at subterfuge. She will sell you things that are harmful but packaged in a lovely outfit. It is like putting a bomb inside a soft toy. No matter how cuddly the toy is, what's inside is deadly. Jezebel was not just a person who lived in Elijah's day. The Bible refers to her as a demonic power.

In Revelation 2:20 we read:
Nevertheless, I have this against you: you tolerate that woman Jezebel, who calls herself a prophet. By her teaching she misleads my servants into sexual immorality and the eating of food sacrificed to idols.

Every time you see Jezebel you will see sexual immorality, because that is an area of weakness that she hammers on.

The Bible says she calls herself a prophetess, and her plan is to prophesy into human hearts, appealing to sensual pride and lustful thoughts. Many people have problems with that area of weakness in the first place. Coupled with Jezebel's influence, it's like fire meeting fire. Jezebel is interested in music that prophesies, movies that prophesy, arts that prophesy, sports that prophesy.

In other words, prophesying is her aim. She is declaring her own message through all those channels. She is Lucifer's right-hand person, since he himself was the chief musician in heaven. Jezebel is his tool to dispense all the vices in his heart.

2 Chronicles 5:1-14 shows how music can create mood in a positive way. They were playing music, and the Bible says the temple was filled with the glory of God so that even the priest could not stand. That is the positive influence of the right kind of music. Music had the profound effect of bringing the glory of God into the temple.

Music can change your mood because it is prophesying into your mind and spirit. So be careful what kind of music you allow into your heart. Music can promote a certain lifestyle and emotional state, and so we need to be watchful. There is no innocent music from Jezebel; she also uses fashion as a key influence and driver for the devil. The church has for so long abandoned this mountain completely, yet most of our youth are influenced by Jezebel's fashion prophecies. A high proportion of fashion designers and trend setters are homosexuals, as Jezebel has been given a free pass to rule this mountain unchallenged.

Jezebel seeks to combine fashion with movies and music for maximum control of the trends. Music in itself will influence, as well as fashion and movies, but when the three combine to create a sub-culture, you have a potent tool that will influence any generation.

An example of the powerful combination of fashion and music is the gothic sub-culture. Here a type of music combines with a fashion style to disseminate Jezebel's message of death, self-hatred, lust, depression and gloom.
Many people, even in the church, buy into this trend without knowing they have become disseminators of Jezebel's prophetic doom messages. It is important we understand this as the enemy's tool.

How to reclaim this mountain
As in the days of old, the dominant spiritual grace that confronts Jezebel is the office of the Prophet. Just as the prophet dealt with Jezebel back then, only people with prophetic grace can

deal with her now.

If we are in these industries, we need to pray, "God give me the prophetic grace to influence this sector." Prophets are known for declaring the heartbeat of God and what is yet to be, and that's what trendsetters are doing with fashion and music. They decide what people are going to be wearing long before it impacts the society, and many people just follow.

The Prophetic Company must rise to confront Jezebel's spirit. God is releasing and revealing sound and sight that will cause people to stand in awe of the Kingdom. That's why groups like *Hillsong* are not just ordinary music groups. Their songs usher us into God's throne room and glorify Christ in our lives. Some musicians seem to have a way of connecting with heaven, and we need to learn to listen to and promote them.

If we set your own trend as led by the Spirit of God, others will follow. Then we'll create our own sub-culture.

We need to reclaim, and the strategies are:
- *Pray for more believers to be released* into this mountain.
- *Pray for prophetic grace* to be released on those called into this arena, that they

would have the boldness to create and the strength to resist the deception of Jezebel.
- *Pray for more awareness in the church* of the vital role of this mountain of Arts and Entertainment and the need to reclaim it for God. If a drama group comes to our church and demonstrates a message of the gospel, and I spend one hour preaching it, most people will remember the play more than my message.

Arts and Entertainment reach our heart. We remember them more. That's why a child can sing a lyric which would fill a page if written down. Yet the same child would not remember a two-line definition out of a school textbook.

We need to move all altars of darkness, not just externally but also internally. This means we need to cleanse ourselves of any influence of Jezebel, because we cannot overcome Jezebel if we are already slaves to her. We must rid ourselves of this satanic influence so that we can begin to dominant this area.

Those chosen and called, it's time to ascend the hill of the Lord with the mind of Christ. God will give you fresh ideas and new trends to set. Don't just copy them. People will then ask, "How did you get this inspiration?"

You will be able to tell them God gave it to you, and you will begin to promote the Kingdom of God that way. Only support those who are promoting God's agenda and advancing the Kingdom. The mountain is to be used to make God famous, not you.

Everything must point back to God. For those who are in this sector, people will try to praise you — even make you demi-gods — but you must constantly direct people upward to God because he is the only one who deserves the praise. Hallelujah!

You will succeed in Jesus name. Do not be afraid. It is time to unleash the creativity of God in this vital sector. That is needed for kingdom take-over.

Note here your Key Learning Points from Chapter 11

CHAPTER 12

BREAKTHROUGH STRATEGIES IN THE RELIGION/RELIGIOUS ARENA

Mountain #6

In this chapter; we will be looking at Religion and the Perizzites. The mountain of Religion is the one most Christians are familiar with. In fact for some it's the only mountain they've known all their lives. It is perhaps the only battle ground that most have recognized.

Many believers think that spiritual warfare happens in a building called "church." They don't understand that in their work place, schools, supermarkets and everywhere else, spiritual warfare is taking place. They are more sensitized to the need and presence of spiritual activities in a religious environment.

> *"When the Lord your God brings you into the land you are entering to possess and drives out before you many nations – the Hittites, Girgashites, Amorites, Canaanites, **Perizzites**, Hivites… seven nations larger and stronger than you …"* **–Deuteronomy 7:1**

The church has brought the gospel of salvation through crusades and outreach events that have helped millions to make decisions to be born again, and that is a good thing.

But as I have shown in the earlier chapters of this book, there is a disconnect between religiosity and good governance. So we find that the most religious nations on earth also have the highest cases of corruption and occult practices. So the church's focus on salvation alone has failed to build up the Kingdom mindset needed to confront the mountain of Religion and present the true reality of Christ.

It is possible for a place to be packed full of people that are born again but whose systems, practices and lifestyles have not been transformed. So we have to move from the gospel of salvation to the gospel of the Kingdom, and take territories.

In other words, now that we are saved, what happens next?

God gave Moses a clear instruction.

"Go to Pharaoh," He said, *"and tell Pharaoh to let my people go, that they may serve me."*

The Bible tells us that after the children of Israel left Egypt and passed through the Red Sea, as over dry land, the Egyptians trying to follow them perished.

It soon became clear, however, that even though they had been released, many of them did not understand why. Not long afterwards they began to worship idols, and something similar has happened in the church today.

We have people who have left Egypt so that they might serve God, the only true God. But Egypt has not left them. Like the ancient Israelites, people in the church have been busy worshipping idols.

People are saved but they do not have an understanding of their mission as the church of Christ. Getting saved is only the first step in the occupation of territories.

As noted in the dictionary, religion is "the service and worship of God or the supernatural, a specific or fundamental set of beliefs and practices generally agreed upon by a number of persons or a sect."

Based on the dictionary definition, we have major world religions such as Christianity, Buddhism, Islam and Hinduism, and we will look at some of them in a moment.

The above definition makes us aware that the mountain of religion is not just about Christianity. Other major religions feature in the landscape too.

Then we have traditional beliefs such as sun worship and all sorts of things. They will not be our focus, but the reclamation principles apply to them as well.

Dominant ruling principality
Who rules the mountain of Religion? Based on Deuteronomy chapter 7, it's the Perizzites. A Perizzite is an "un-walled or rustic dweller." Un-walled suggests a lack of protection.

In Joshua 17:14-15 we read:
Then the children of Joseph spoke to Joshua, saying, "Why have you given us only one lot and one share to inherit, since we are a great people, inasmuch as the Lord has blessed us until now?" So Joshua answered them, "If you are a great people, then go up to the forest country and clear a place for yourself there in

*the land of the **Perizzites** and the giants, since the mountains of Ephraim are too confined for you."*

The **Perizzites** and the giants represent idolatry. Notice that they said Mount Ephraim was too confined for them, so they wanted something special in addition. In the Scriptures, idolatry was always entrenched in high places.
In a famous song by Ron Kenoly are the words: "We're going up to the high places to tear the devil's kingdom down." So the Perizzites dwell in high places where idolatry and false worship occur.

The Perizzites also lived in the land of giants, and we know idolatry creates religious giants that need to be removed. Some time ago I was watching a documentary on scientology. I could not believe how somebody who started out as a science fiction writer turned his stories into a religion in which people now believed in aliens.
I asked myself, *what happened here?*

Idolatry strips people of their protection and provision and makes them subservient to false gods. History shows that as a people begin to eradicate idolatry and turn to the worship of the true God, a better economy and less war always follow. The correlation between godly people and better living standards is a constant in

Scripture. Transforming a nation is not just about improving its productive capacity; it's about improving its spiritual climate as well.

Idolatry is the worship of a physical object as a god. Or it can be simply an attachment or devotion to something. The first definition refers to a spiritual activity but the second suggests anything we become attached to can become an idols for us — a phone, gadget, car or anything else.

Some people make an idol of the club they support, because if a game falls within church time, church will be skipped that day. When God takes second place to our other passions, there is a spiritual dimension involved.

Did you know there is a religion around Elvis Presley? I have seen a documentary of people gathering to worship Elvis. People do crazy things. An idol is an object of worship, a likeness of something, a false god, a pretender or an imposter. There are many potential idols in our lives and much religion is based on idol worship.

Let's look at some key religions I mentioned earlier. I will not go into detail but present an overview.

Islam

In Islam the central idolatry is the worship of Allah. Whoever they intend to worship I don't know but their actual god seems to be connected with the Prince of Persia that Daniel dealt with. As far as I am concerned the god they worship and my own God are not the same. I've heard a former archbishop of Canterbury and some other ministers calling for more unity. "After all, we all worship the same God," they say. "We just worship him differently."

I'm sorry but we *don't* all worship the same God. The Bible makes it clear that no one comes to the Father except through Jesus Christ. The Bible says that human righteousness is like filthy rags so there is no way we can have access to our heavenly Father if we have not been cleansed by the blood of the Lamb. How can we say Jesus is *not* the Saviour of the world and yet want to relate with God directly? It is not possible.

I agree we ought to be at peace with each other, but we don't have to claim falsely that we all worship the same God.

The central idolatry in Islam is the worship of a man called Muhammad. You can see that he's an idol because if you dare to represent him in a cartoon or write something about him that Muslims don't like, they will put a fatwa on you. Violence or threats of violence have now cowed even the liberal Western press into not saying anything against Islam.

They are now censoring themselves, the same press that wouldn't blink an eye to tell you Jesus was gay and insult Christianity for fun. The press / media / arts sector are happy to poke fun at Christianity in comedy shows, but when it comes to Islam they know not to go there. It's too dangerous.

The reason Christians don't fight back is simple: a God who cannot defend himself is not worth serving. I don't think it is my job to go out and kill people on behalf of God. The Bible says "'Vengeance is mine', saith the Lord." With these words he seems to be saying, "Don't bother fighting on my behalf."

So even if you shout abuse at me that Jesus is a criminal, I will just tell you that God will deal with you himself, because God will do more to you than I ever could. After all, the weapons of our warfare are not carnal but mighty through God. It is not that Christians are weak, but that God through us will use the foolish things of this world to confound the wise.

Through the foolishness of preaching; we must reclaim the mountain of religion until the world declares, as the king did in the days of Daniel, that our God is the only true God.

As we are seeing with fundamentalist Islam and its violence, Satan is finding willing hearts and minds to use in these groups to shed innocent blood and entrench his slant of religion on the face of the earth. The Final battle for hearts and minds have begun. But through God we shall do crush the enemy, because it is He who works in us to do valiantly as we advance His purpose on the earth.

Hinduism
Hinduism is the most idolatrous religion on earth. It has more than three hundred million gods and counting. Hindus sell their souls to an array of demons who are then empowered to rule among them. Most Hindus are open to anything. They accept any new god that could grant them favour. That's why animals — especially cows — are objects of worship, and in places where Hinduism is dominant they hardly kill any animals.

In Indian cows are sacred, so even if they contracted an infectious illness like mad cow disease, the people would prefer to go mad than kill the cow. Hinduism is idolatrous, but this also means some people may be easier to reach with the gospel, if we prayerfully prepare ourselves, because they are open to anything supernatural. They are especially open if we can demonstrate the power of God to them.

Buddhism
The central idol in Buddhism is the *self*. The individual's path to salvation is through works, meditation and self-discipline. It's about transcending thoughts; it's about practising yoga and enlightening the mind. Buddhists don't believe in God or in any supernatural object out there, but they tend to be open to new spiritual possibilities from any source whatsoever.

They are like a confluence of spiritual experiments. So they too are filled with idols and images, and are only marginally behind the Hindus in respect of how many things they idolise.

That's why you will see Buddhists with lots of ornaments and paraphernalia around them, including statues. It's all about self and meditation.

There are many other forms of idolatry in the world, from Chinese and African traditional religions to witchcraft and voodoo. Witchcraft is a particularly interesting one because there are people who call themselves good witches. That's like talking about good devils.

Some people call themselves "white witches," meaning they don't do bad things like other witches. They get their power from the devil but they don't do evil. Does that make sense?

Let us be clear: the number one objective of all these faiths that are based on the mountain of religion (remember I haven't mentioned Christianity yet) is to *direct to themselves the worship meant for the true God.* As a result, many of these demons don't mind the use of the Bible as a pretence to advance their falsehoods. Just because a group carries the Bible around, this does not mean it is godly.

The logic of Satan is: if using the Bible will bring more people for the demons to inhabit that's fine. That's why we see some people in the church using these evil powers, as well as using the Bible at their meetings.

Remember each temptation of Jesus in the wilderness? Each time the devil began with a quotation from the Bible, but twisted it. He knows the Bible too, you know!

It is possible to see ungodly ministers going around with Bibles. Don't be deceived by them.

It is by their fruits that we shall know them. Jesus talked about some people who would call him "Lord, Lord!" He said he would respond to them, "Who are you? I don't know you! Depart from me, you workers of iniquity."

When we see things like this happening, we should not be surprised. We can see the handwriting on the wall, based on what has already been declared. We all need discernment to identify the falsehoods.

Who Rules over this Mountain?

The principality sitting on top of this mountain is what I call a "religious spirit." Satan himself is actually controlling things on the mountain but I call it a religious spirit because it manifests itself in different ways. There is not one particular demon in charge of religion but a collective we term religious spirits as there are minor differences between each religion.

You must first of all understand that true Christianity is not a religion. It is a lifestyle. You have to reflect Christ in all that you do.

These demons are assigned to steal the worship that is designated for God. Satan, you recall, was the anointed cherub. He was in charge of music and worship in heaven. But one of the things that sent him packing was his desire to become the object of worship.

He has been manifesting himself in every religion ever since. He's still stealing the worship designated for God and trying to direct it towards himself. We human beings have a sort of innate homing device which causes us to seek God and to know him. The job of the religious spirit is to sabotage our homing device and lead the worship elsewhere. He takes advantage of our desire to seek God and brings a substitute our way.

Manifestations of the religious spirit

How does the religious spirit steal worship that belongs to God?

There are seven ways:
1. *He inspires an open intentional worship of Satan.* This is called Satanism and its adherents call themselves Satanists. They worship Satan openly.
2. *He diverts worship to idols that originate in his mind* and he gives them different names. These objects form the basis of many religions in the world.
3. *He diverts worship to man.* Here he doesn't get the worship himself, but he knows that the worship of the self displeases God, so he is happy with it. Here it is usually about the mind.

4. *He makes worship vague and symbolic.* If God must be worshiped at all, the devil allows self-made religion that excludes Jesus. The Bible can be used in worship, but Christ is not the access point. There are many denominations that call themselves Christian who do not believe in Christ as the Saviour of the world.

5. *If a relationship with God via Jesus Christ is present, then doctrinally he will eliminate the Holy Spirit.* He started with unadulterated satanic worship and then realized it wouldn't sell in many territories. So he began to mix up his methods so it became less obvious who was behind them. We see this in the biblical account of Apollos, who at first didn't know about the Holy Spirit. In the past many Christian denominations have not believed in the baptism of the Holy Spirit. Satan has been behind this.

6. *If a relationship with God through Christ and the Holy Spirit is present, he then eliminates power manifestations.* He starts from a non-God perspective, and when he sees he's not getting his way he tries to minimise the manifestations of God's glory. In some churches he promotes a powerless gospel.

7. If a true relationship with God through Jesus is present, one that includes power manifestations of the Holy Spirit (in which case the gospel seems to be complete), *he then obscures the theological understanding of how*

close we can get to God and how much authority we have been given on earth. His objective is to promote ignorance of dominion authority.

This means the religious spirit has created what I call "immobilized rapture waiters," people who do not impact any territory and are not reclaiming any mountain in the marketplace. They believe in God, Jesus, and the power of the Holy Spirit and its manifestations, but they don't understand their mission on earth.

These frozen saints make Satan happy. He is content for us to be having our little meetings, as long as we are just sitting and waiting for the end to come. Meanwhile we are leaving him unchallenged on all the mountains.

In these seven points there is no religion you won't find, from pure satanic worship to a pure church that is immobilized.

Tools of deception
The following list of tools and methods of the religious spirit is not exhaustive, but the key ones include:

1. *Fear of people.* This manifests in two ways. Either you are always trying to please people rather than God, and so

you fear what others might say, or you fear people so much that you cannot tell them what God wants you to say. You'd rather tell them what they want to hear.
2. *Approval is sought through works and not grace.*
3. *External things are emphasized*, leading to carnality and legalism.
4. *False ways and false prophecies* abound.
5. *Human doctrines, commandments and traditions* are emphasized.
6. There is *pride in personal sacrifice or discipline*, and a *lack of mercy.*

Reclaim Authority

The prevailing authority to reclaim this mountain is not found in any human office. It is the Holy Spirit himself. For some of the mountains we have looked at we have prophetic grace and the like, but the only way to dismantle the mountain of religion is the Holy Spirit of God. This means it is the job of every believer the Holy Spirit is working through.

I can understand why this is so, because some of the greatest obstacles to the progress of the gospel and the take-over of the marketplace are pastors. So if God were to place the reclaiming assignment on pastors alone, we'd be in trouble.

How do we take over this mountain?

Only true worshippers can dare to go after this mountain of religion. True worshippers need to rise up and displace false worship by prayer and intercession for the destruction and removal of the religious spirit.

The true church will need to confront the religious spirit holding people captive in churches as well as in other religions. If you read the book of Jeremiah carefully, especially the first half, you will see God's warning about bad shepherds that are not leading his people aright.

We need to understand that part of the problem in the true church today are the shepherds as well as the sheep.

What will happen when we take over this mountain?

1. The blinding power behind many of these religions will be shattered and captives will be set free.
2. Many will defect over to the Lord's side into true worship. They'll be tired of false worship.
3. The last enemy to be taken down from this mountain is that which calls itself "Christian" but which operates only according to human wisdom.

What the Holy Spirit instils and installs once he shows up on this mountain is:

1. **GOD'S CHARACTER:** that is, the fruit of the Holy Spirit (Galatians 5:22-23).
2. **GOD'S POWER:** that is, the gift of the Holy Spirit (1 Corinthians 12:1-11)
3. **GOD'S STRUCTURE:** that is, the five-fold ministry of the church (Ephesians 4:11-13). The true church will then return to the scriptural pattern set by God himself.

This is what the Holy Spirit will do as a way of returning the church to its scriptural pattern. Isaiah 2:2, 8, 17, 18, 19, 20 and 21 is recommended reading. We can see that God is coming to reclaim this mountain by himself in full power.

All these scriptures show that we cannot take this mountain without the help of God. This means he will go before us. We need to position ourselves accurately, and the true church will then emerge without spot or wrinkle, as the Bible has declared.

The good news is, God has *already* gone ahead of us. It is now our turn to follow as the true church of the living God.

Note here your Key Learning Points from Chapter 12

CHAPTER 13

BREAKTHROUGH STRATEGIES IN <u>FAMILY</u> LIFE

Mountain #7

This is the last of the seven sectors (mountains of culture) in the marketplace. We have considered the Media, Government, Education, Economy, Arts and Entertainment and Religion, now we look at the Family.

If you look at these seven sectors, you will see they cover the entire nation state. Everything fits into one of the seven categories.

"When the Lord your God brings you into the land which you go to possess, and has cast out many nations before you, the Hittites and the Girgashites and the Amorites and the Canaanites and the Perizzites and the Hivites and the Jebusites, seven nations greater and

*mightier than you… **Deuteronomy 7:1-4***

In this chapter, we will examine the Jebusite spirit and its effect on the mountain of Family.

Malachi 4:5-6 says: *"Behold, I will send you Elijah the prophet before the coming of the great and dreadful day of the Lord. And he will turn the hearts of the fathers to the children, and the hearts of the children to their fathers, lest I come and strike the earth with a curse."*

Saving families is a key objective of God in the last days. God will restore the position of fatherhood as never before. We live amidst unprecedented family breakdown. The family unit is clearly under assault by Satan and the family is being constantly redefined. It is the fathers who have failed in many of these cases, although there are other factors as well.

In the last days so much evil will be released that some children will even turn against their parents. Not everything that is happening can be viewed from a natural vantage point. Some things we have to look at from a supernatural perspective.

Children will rise against their parents. The media are full of reports of children killing their parents in the USA and other countries. This unprecedented evil is taking place in our generation, as well as cases of parents killing their children.

All these shocking things come from satanic influences. So we need to fight the battle to save families. And we need to understand how God is going to intervene.

"But know this, that in the last days perilous times will come: For men will be lovers of themselves, lovers of money, boasters, proud, blasphemers, **disobedient to parents, unthankful**, *unholy, unloving, unforgiving, slanderers, without self-control, brutal, despisers of good, traitors, headstrong, haughty, lovers of pleasure rather than lovers of God."* **2 Timothy 3:1-4**

Some of these behaviours that will become prevalent in some children in the last days. Yet the Bible is clear that fathers and mothers are to be honoured so that our days may be long.

Disobedience to parent is a serious matter and a sign of the end times. We will see children who are ungrateful for what their parents or caregivers have done for them. Unforgiving and without self-control.

This could be substance-related, such as taking

drugs, getting drunk and losing self-restraint. All these things will happen in the last days.

The family is an institution created by God as the very foundation of all societies. Every function of society is based on the family. When the family disintegrates, the social order also disintegrates.

In America, the 1987 *Survey of Youth in Custody* found that 70 percent of incarcerated youth did not grow up with both parents. A 1994 study of the State of Wisconsin juveniles was even starker.

Only 13 percent grew up with their married parents. Here is the conclusion of Cynthia Harper and Sara McLanahan, researchers on single parenthood:

"Controlling for income and all other factors, youths in father-absent families (mother only, mother-stepfather, and relatives/other) still had significantly higher odds of incarceration than those from mother-father families."

These statistics illustrate the damaging effect of family breakdown and the absence of fathers. This doesn't mean that being a single-parent family is bad in every sense.

But it does mean that the absence of fathers

can cause problems, especially if there are no other male figures around to compensate. In some situations three generations of a family are in jail, the grandfather, father and grandson. In fact there is a case in the US where all of them are in the same prison!

So it's important to look at the issue of family. Please note that I am generalising from the statistics. Single parent families happen for all kinds of reasons, not all of them by choice. If you have a man and he decides to clear out, what can you do other than to pray?

Some single-parent families are doing fine. In fact many single parents are doing a brilliant job. But the ideal is still a stable, two-parent (Mum and Dad) family

Who rules this mountain?
The Jebusite spirit rules over the mountain of Families. Jebusite means downtrodden or rejected. This is what we must displace. Rejection is what drives families apart, just as love binds them together.

Couples can feel rejected as well as other family members, and this can be caused by misunderstandings. Often we interpret others' words through the prism of what we are going through rather than hearing what the other is really saying. Rejection can easily result.

A Jebusite will take advantage of every opening to sow rejection. And this is the foundation of strife.

The principality that sits on top of this mountain is called Baal. Baal is one of the most evil manifestations of the devilish powers. Baal and Jezebel are similar; Jezebel serves Baal. Baal means master, owner or Lord, all expressions for Satan.

Baal is a powerful manifestation of evil. He was the god of fertility, the sun god, the god of rain and the god of provision. He was looked to for basically everything. So it was as if the entire pagan nation depended on Baal for its provision.

The cult of Baal usually included male prostitution. Baal worship included service to the god *Molech*.
"And they built the high places of Baal which are in the Valley of the Son of Hinnom, to cause their sons and their daughters to pass through the fire to Molech, which I did not command them, nor did it come into my mind that they should do this abomination, to cause Judah to sin." **–Jeremiah 32:35.**

Believe it or not, Baal worship exists today in many forms, and you'll see how it has entered into world leaders. If you Google the phrase *Bohemian Grove* you'll see it's a place in California where key world leaders gather annually.

Ten years ago a Christian guy in the US infiltrated them and spent about four hours in there, unknown to them. He showed how the place was guarded by the CIA and revealed many of the things the leaders did. He actually captured some of them on video, performing Baal worship. Do the research and make up your own mind. It appears to be a cult that engages in satanic rituals.

Some researchers claim that in both the Republican and the Democratic parties nobody has become President in the last 100 years that has not visited Bohemian Grove. They have to endorse you, it seems.

You can do your own research on this, but the point I'm making is that the worship of Baal has not died. It's still going strong, and I believe it is behind many of the evil manifestations we are seeing.

There is a huge sexual undertone to Baal worship generally, and religious prostitution was even commanded. Human sacrifices were also common. In an effort to placate their god the people would kill young children and bury them in the foundation of a house or public building at the time of its construction.

You can see that curse declared in Joshua 6:26: *Then Joshua charged them at that time, saying, "Cursed be the man before the Lord who rises up and builds this city Jericho; he shall lay its foundation with his firstborn, and with his youngest he shall set up its gates."*

So Baal worship was a powerful attraction to the children of Israel and eventually led to their destruction and exile. The northern kingdom of Israel wanted idolatry and the Lord gave them over to Assyria.

The southern kingdom of Israel wanted idolatry and the Lord gave them over to Babylon. Both lands were filled to the brim with idolatry. The religion of Baal, or Molech as it manifest itself, is very bad.

Molech demanded the cruel and brutal sacrifice of children. They did this either by killing the children and burying them, or by making Molech statues out of metal which they would heat up to become red hot. Live children would be placed on the statue and parents would watch as their child was burnt to death.

Is there a link between the sacrifice of children in Baal worship and the prevalence of abortions today? Modern nations are killing their children through liberal abortion policies.

Homosexuality is also a manifestation of Baal worship, which explains why male prostitution is integral to Baal ceremonies. As Baal is crushed, then, the homosexual spirit will weaken and many will flock to the church for deliverance and acceptance.

I hope you'll begin to see how Baal has infiltrated the church. Baal worship is not just male sexual activity. It's about base sexual activity generally. All kinds of unthinkable sexual activities take place in Baal worship.

Pastors (ministry gift) and pastoral grace are the dominant spiritual authority to defeat Baal because people need to be cared for. Anticipating this, Baal has forcefully sent his demons to infect many pastors because he knows that pastoral grace is needed to defeat him.

That is why you will see many pastors being exposed as homosexual practitioners in the days to come. For Baal, attack is the best form of defence. So he is forcibly sending his demons to buffet many pastors, create confusion, and undermine God's plan. But he will not succeed.

The church must be ready for many pastors to be exposed as being under Baal's influence of debased sexual practices. So when you hear of this in the coming days and months, don't be shocked. It is God's move to cleanse his church. God is beginning the cleansing.

Psalm 68:5-6 says:
"A father of the fatherless, a defender of widows, is God in his holy habitation. God sets the solitary in families; he brings out those who are bound into prosperity; but the rebellious dwell in a dry land."

The words "father of the fatherless" mean that God's heart is that of a family man. He knows some fathers will walk away and some families will be without fathers, so to balance things up he said he would become a father to the fatherless. Knowing that some would lose their fathers, he has chosen to fill the void.

So God will not leave us in a rejected state. Man might have rejected us but God will not reject us. Man might walk out on us but God will not walk out on us. Man might have divorced us, but

God will not divorce us. Regardless of the mistakes we might have made in the past, God says he will not leave us in a rejected state.

He sets the solitary in families. If we don't have a family, God will find one for us. We might be an orphan and have no one, but God says he will surround us with people who will act as a family for us. God understands that we need that setup to be able to move to the next level.

How do we reclaim the mountain of the family?
The marketplace cannot be complete if families are not complete. We need two key strategies:
1. **Prayer:** We need to begin consistent prayers for the family as part of our individual prayer time. Remember families individually and corporately. We need to pray constantly against Baal and his manifestations.
2. **Action:** We need to work on family cohesion. This means believers need to invade the structures of Babylon that deal with families. We need believers to become social workers who make decisions over families. We need believers to occupy those positions because these are people who by one simple signature can tear families apart. As Christians reclaim all the other mountains, we will have believers in places of authority who will influence family policies in our nations.

So we need both a prayer strategy and an action strategy to dislodge Baal from the mountain of families. If we don't break through in the spiritual realm first, we will not win in the physical.

First and foremost we need to pray, because Baal's influence needs to be weakened. Baal and Jezebel are a tough combination.

For example, there are politicians both in Africa and the West that Baal controls through women. Women make a covenant with Baal and then look for a politician to sleep with. Once that happens there is nothing the politicians won't say yes to. This is just one of the ways Baal uses lust and sexual perversion to control people in power.

We are fighting spiritual battles. That is why it's not always the most qualified who get the jobs or who get elected into office. And those who get elected may not be particularly deserving.

Mantle to reclaim this mountain
Who are the kinds of people we need who will reclaim this mountain? A Joseph generation will emerge who will have the grace and enablement to confront this it. We must all pass the Potiphar's wife test before we can access Pharaoh's palace.

Joseph was subjected to Potiphar's wife's advances. And they didn't happen just once. He was subjected to them day by day for a period of time. So too the new Josephs will be subjected to this test every day in every mountain of the marketplace. The Potiphar's wife test is designed to distract us and change our focus.

If you are on the mountain of business, your test might consist of repeated attempts to corrupt you. Will you be corrupted? It will not be a one-time event. If you are on the mountain of family, repeated attempts will be made to corrupt you sexually and mess you up.

So you must ensure you pass the Potiphar's wife test. God bless you.

Note here your Key Learning Points from Chapter 13

CHAPTER 14

BECOMING A MOUNTAIN TAKER

God created man to have dominion over all the earth. Dominion speaks of Kingdom or domain. Man lost it at Eden, but in Christ, the dominion or rulership of the Kingdom is restored to us.

"Until John the Baptist began to preach, the laws of Moses and the messages of the prophets were your guides. But now the Good News of the Kingdom of God is preached, and eager multitudes are forcing their way in. ¹⁷But that doesn't mean that the law has lost its force in even the smallest point. It is stronger and more permanent than heaven and earth. **–Luke 16 [NLT]**

Up until John the Baptist, the Law of Moses was fully operational. The people also had the books of the prophets (all announcing the coming of the King, the Messiah).

The first five books of the Bible are known as the "Pentateuch" or the "Books of Moses." These are;

Genesis – Creation, the fall, sin, how Israel came to be a nation and then came to be in Egypt.
Exodus – The deliverance of the people of Israel from slavery in Egypt.
Leviticus – The book of the Law.
Numbers – The wandering in the wilderness.
Deuteronomy – Israel prepares to move into the Promised Land.

The *books of the Law* are the first five books of the Bible. From Joshua to Malachi, the *books of the prophetic writings* all speak about Jesus.

The master confirms this himself on the road to Emmaus:
Luke 24:13-27
[13] Now behold, two of them were travelling that same day to a village called Emmaus, which was seven miles from Jerusalem. [14]And they talked together of all these things which had happened. [15]So it was, while they conversed

and reasoned, that Jesus himself drew near and went with them. ¹⁶But their eyes were restrained, so that they did not know him.

¹⁷And he said to them, "What kind of conversation is this that you have with one another as you walk and are sad?" ¹⁸Then the one whose name was Cleopas answered and said to him, "Are you the only stranger in Jerusalem, and have you not known the things which happened there in these days?"

¹⁹And he said to them, "What things?" So they said to him, "The things concerning Jesus of Nazareth, who was a Prophet mighty in deed and word before God and all the people, ²⁰and how the chief priests and our rulers delivered him to be condemned to death, and crucified him. ²¹But we were hoping that it was he who was going to redeem Israel. Indeed, besides all this, today is the third day since these things happened. ²²Yes, and certain women of our company, who arrived at the tomb early, astonished us. ²³When they did not find his body, they came saying that they had also seen a vision of angels who said he was alive. ²⁴And certain of those who were with us went to the tomb and found it just as the women had said; but him they did not see." ²⁵Then he said to them, "O foolish ones, and slow of heart to believe in all that the prophets have spoken! ²⁶Ought not the Christ to have suffered these things and to enter into his glory?" ²⁷And

beginning at Moses and all the Prophets, he expounded to them in all the Scriptures the things concerning himself.

Christ is the theme of the entire revelation of God's word. He is promised in Genesis, revealed in the law, prefigured in its history, praised in its poetry, proclaimed in its prophecy provided in its Gospels, proved in its Acts, pre-eminent in its Epistles and prevailing in Revelation.

He is seen in every verse and every book of the Bible. In many types and shadows, Christ was revealed in the Old Testament. *More than one representation of him exists in each book,* but let's take a look at a typical depiction of Christ in the Bible. It's a matter of personal revelation.

[16]Let your light so shine before men, that they may see your good works and glorify your Father in heaven. [17] "Do not think that I came to destroy the Law or the Prophets. I did not come to destroy but to fulfill. [18]For assuredly, I say to you, till heaven and earth pass away, one jot or one tittle will by no means pass from the law till all is fulfilled. **– Matthew 5:16-17**

"Then he said to them, "These are the words which I spoke to you while I was still with you, that all things must be fulfilled which were

*written in the **Law** of Moses and the **Prophets** and the Psalms concerning me."* –**Luke 24:44**

After his temptations in the wilderness and at the start of his ministry, Jesus declared: *"Repent, for the kingdom of heaven is at hand."* –**Matthew 4:17**

He said to them, "I must preach the kingdom of God to the other cities also, because for this purpose I have been sent." –**Luke 4:43**

To finally confirm this, Jesus took three of his disciples to witness a handover ceremony:

Matthew 17:1-13
*1 Now after six days Jesus took Peter, James, and John his brother, led them up on a high mountain by themselves; 2and he was transfigured before them. His face shone like the sun, and his clothes became as white as the light. 3And behold, Moses and Elijah appeared to them, talking with him. 4Then Peter answered and said to Jesus, "Lord, it is good for us to be here; if you wish, let us make here three tabernacles: one for you, one for Moses, and one for Elijah."
5While he was still speaking,* (God shut him and his religious spirit up) *behold, a bright cloud overshadowed them; and suddenly a voice came out of the cloud, saying, "This is my*

beloved Son, in whom I am well pleased. Hear him!" ⁶And when the disciples heard it, they fell on their faces and were greatly afraid. ⁷But Jesus came and touched them and said, "Arise, and do not be afraid." ⁸When they had lifted up their eyes, they saw no one but Jesus only. (The Law and the prophet were gone). ⁹Now as they came down from the mountain, Jesus commanded them, saying, "Tell the vision to no one until the Son of Man is risen from the dead." ¹⁰And his disciples asked him, saying, "Why then do the scribes say that Elijah must come first?"

¹¹Jesus answered and said to them, "Indeed, Elijah is coming first and will restore all things. ¹²But I say to you that Elijah has come already, and they did not know him but did to him whatever they wished. Likewise the Son of Man is also about to suffer at their hands." ¹³Then the disciples understood that he spoke to them of John the Baptist.

(See also Mal. 4:1-5, Luke 1:11-17)

Key points to note:
- This meeting on the mountain was not just about transfiguration. It was also about *transferring*.
- Jesus "picked up the baton," so to speak, from Moses (the Law) and Elijah (the Prophets).

- **Luke 16 [NLT]** - *[16]"Until John the Baptist began to preach, the laws of Moses and the messages of the prophets were your guides. But now the good news of the Kingdom of God is preached,*
- The conversation on the mount between Moses, Elijah and Jesus was about the closure of one assignment and the start of a new one, the gospel of the Kingdom.
- Peter had a religious spirit which afflicts many churches today. He wanted to build monuments to the dead. Many of us are busy building such monuments, but God is not in it.
- A voice came from heaven confirming the transfer that had just taken place. But when the disciples looked, it was only Jesus that remained. Now the Law and the Prophets have had their day. Jesus is the only one we must now preach.
- Before John the Baptist, all that could be preached was the Law and the Prophets. But when Jesus came, the prophecies were fulfilled and the law was fulfilled under a new grace of God.

John 1:45 – *Philip found Nathanael and said to him, "We have found him of whom Moses in the **law**, and also the **prophets**, wrote--Jesus of Nazareth, the son of Joseph."*

Romans 3:21- *But now the righteousness of God apart from the* **law** *is revealed, being witnessed by the* **law** *and the* **prophets**,

From now on we are mandated to preach only the *gospel of the kingdom,* and to reign on earth like kings, exercising authority and dominion over all things. Jesus has conferred on us the kingship of this kingdom:

Daniel 7:18 - *[18] But the saints of the Most High will receive the kingdom and will possess it forever—yes, for ever and ever.'*

Luke 22:29 – *[29] "And I bestow upon you a kingdom, just as my Father bestowed one upon me, [30]that you may eat and drink at my table in my kingdom, and sit on thrones judging the twelve tribes of Israel."*

Luke 12:32- *[32]"Do not fear, little flock, for it is your Father's good pleasure to give you the kingdom".*

A kingdom is a governing authority that influences its territories. If we understand what the kingdom is, we will then be able to understand who the kings of the kingdom should be and the keys with which to enter it.

Isaiah 9:6-7 - *For unto us a Child is born, unto*

us a Son is given; and the government will be upon his shoulder. And his name will be called Wonderful, Counsellor, Mighty God, Everlasting Father, Prince of Peace. Of the increase of his government and peace there will be no end. Upon the throne of David and over his kingdom, to order it and establish it with judgment and justice from that time forward, even forever. The zeal of the Lord of hosts will perform this.

Kingdom dominion is about citizenship and governance. The *kingdom of heaven* is a place which we can experience from the earth, while the *kingdom of God* is God's way of doing things, his values, his principles --- and therefore his word. The word of God is still the final authority in all things.

Matthew 4 - *[17]From that time Jesus began to preach and to say, "Repent, for the kingdom of heaven is at hand."*

Luke 4 - *[43]but he said to them, "I must preach the kingdom of God to the other cities also, because for this purpose I have been sent."*

So Jesus came to preach the kingdom of God so that we can be ready to receive and enter the kingdom of heaven. We have no business with the kingdom of heaven if we do not live our lives in the kingdom of God.

How can people live in heaven when they do not know God's ways of doing things? The kingdom of God is revealed in the word of God. Obeying the word of God establishes the kingdom of God in us. Obedience to the word of God is the key to rulership in God's kingdom on earth.

Recognizing the voice of the Holy Spirit is the greatest asset to any believer's destiny. Divine guidance is key to reclaiming the marketplace.

Psalm 23:1-6 - *[1] The Lord is my shepherd; I shall not want. [2]He makes me to lie down in green pastures. He leads me beside the still waters. [3]He restores my soul. He leads me in the paths of righteousness for his name's sake. [4]Yea, though I walk through the valley of the shadow of death, I will fear no evil; for you are with me; your rod and your staff, they comfort me. [5]You prepare a table before me in the presence of my enemies. You anoint my head with oil; my cup runs over. [6]Surely goodness and mercy shall follow me all the days of my life; and I will dwell in the house of the Lord forever.*

Products of Divine Guidance from Psalm 23:

PROVISION - Divine guidance commands *divine provision.* – v 1. Just like Elijah in 1 Kings

17.

REST - Divine guidance commands *divine rest.* v 2-3. You will cease struggling, Heb. 4:1-11. Rest is an expression of dominion.

CONFIDENCE: Divine guidance commands *divine confidence.* v 4a. Cast not away your confidence. Isa. 30:15

CONQUEST - Divine guidance commands *divine conquest.* v 4b-5a. God shows you off. Conquest is where your mere presence disarms the enemy.

EMPOWERMENT - Divine guidance commands *divine empowerment.* v 5b Oil represents the anointing.

FAVOUR - Divine guidance commands *divine favour.* v 6a

SECURITY - Divine guidance commands divine security. v 6b

These are the seven instruments of dominion and breakthrough available to all the children of God to possess the seven mountains of culture of nations.

These seven instruments should be present in

your life as you embark on the mission to reclaim the marketplace for the Lord.

Behind every supernatural exploit is divine guidance. The reality of God's power is manifested through obedience to divine direction. Remember, it was God who told Abraham to move. It was God who told Isaac not to go to Egypt, but to Gera. Our provision and victory is at the place of obedience to God's voice.

Isaiah 42:18-24 - *[18]"Oh, how deaf and blind you are toward me! Why won't you listen? Why do you refuse to see? [19]Who in all the world is as blind as my own people, my servant? Who is as deaf as my messengers? Who is as blind as my chosen people, the servant of the LORD? [20]You see and understand what is right but refuse to act on it. You hear, but you don't really listen." [21]The LORD has magnified his law and made it truly glorious. Through it he had planned to show the world that he is righteous. [22]But what a sight his people are, for they have been robbed, enslaved, imprisoned, and trapped. They are fair game for all and have no one to protect them. [23]Will not even one of you apply these lessons from the past and see the ruin that awaits you? [24]Who allowed Israel to be robbed and hurt? Was it not the LORD? It was the LORD whom we sinned against, for the people* *would not go where he sent them, nor would they obey his law.*

When Christians are spiritually deaf or blind, their destiny is a prison. You were born for dominion. You are the light of the world. Obedience to God's word and voice brings dominion and enables us to break through all the opposition in the marketplace. Step out and become all that God wants you to be. God bless you.

Mountain Takers
Joshua chapter 14:6-14 shows us pointers for mountain takers. We must discover where we fit in one of these seven mountains. There are two postures we could have as we take a mountain—serving with the servants or walking with the kings.

If we are on the mountain of politics, for example, walking with the kings could mean being elected to a political post whereas serving with the servants could mean being a political operative, working behind the scenes. We are the special advisers, the ones the king relies on, but people don't know us. So we need to understand which one we are, either the front end or the back end.

We are either a Joshua or a Caleb. For the front

line to take a mountain we must have certain things.

Front office
- We need *great faith*. Numbers 14:6-8
- We must be *consecrated completely* to God. Numbers 32:12
- We must be *spiritually minded*. Joshua 3:5, 8:30.

Remember, after they lost the battle of Ai which was supposed to be a simple battle, Joshua went back to inquire of the Lord what may have gone wrong. He could have analysed their physical strategy to find out why they had lost the battle but he understood there must be a spiritual reason.

When he went to God, God was able to tell him, "Remember I told you not to take anything out of this city? Achan was greedy and took some things from the city, and because of that, innocent people died."

If you have an Achan in your camp, it is not just him or his family who will suffer the consequences but the entire nation.

So we need the following characteristics of Joshua:
- **Godly reference.** Joshua 5:14. You cannot reference his presence if you are not able to

identify his presence.
- **Courage.** Joshua 10:25. Courage is not the absence of fear; it is acting in spite of your fears.
- **Complete obedience.** Joshua 11:16. As far as God is concerned 99 per cent obedience is disobedience.
- **Decisiveness in decision-making.** Joshua 24:15. That's one of the things Joshua learnt from Moses.
- **Christlikeness** in every respect.

Back office
If your role is to operate at the lower level or in the background, you also need certain key qualities. These are:
- Courage
- Perseverance
- Consecration before God
- Vigour and faith regardless of age.
- Invincibility.
- Technical skill

Advice for mountain takers
- Always speak with clear directives.
- Have an understanding of your mission and vision, along with whatever else you need for the assignment.
- Seek circumstances in the light of God.
- Obey God and insist others obey him as well

- Display deep courage and faith in the situation you are in.
- Believe you have been strengthened to acquire the wealth for the next generation.

Three things the enemy uses to entrap mountain takers
- Passion — Focus your passion on God.
- Possession — Avoid greed and materialism
- Position — Live above the pride of life.

Who can God use?
You. Just as you are. You are perfect for what God wants to do. So simply yield yourself to him and see God use you as never before.

Friends, this is the end of our journey in this book. I trust you are now challenged and ready to take your place in God's end-time plan. The marketplace is ripe and we must reclaim it with the force of righteousness. God bless you. See you at the top. Keep winning.

"Now after the three-and-a-half days the breath of life from God entered them, and they stood on their feet, and great fear fell on those who saw them. And they heard a loud voice from heaven saying to them, "Come up here." And they ascended to heaven in a cloud, and their enemies saw them. In the same hour there was a great earthquake, and a tenth of the city fell.

In the earthquake seven thousand people were killed, and the rest were afraid and gave glory to the God of heaven. The second woe is past. Behold, the third woe is coming quickly. Then the seventh angel sounded: And there were loud voices in heaven, saying, **"The kingdoms of this world have become the kingdoms of our Lord and of his Christ***, and he shall reign forever and ever!"* **– Revelation 11:11-15**

So let us go and take the mountains for God. The Marketplace has been redeemed and is now ready…Let the redeemed of the Lord say so.

See you at the top of the mountains. God bless you.

Note here your Key Learning Points from Chapter 14

Note here your Summary Reflections from the entire Book

Note here your Summary Reflections from the entire Book

Books by Charles Omole

- Church, Its time to Fly -- Learning to fly on Eagles Wings
- How to Avoid Getting Hurt in Church -- 13 Steps that will protect you and help create an atmosphere for breakthroughs.
- Must I go to Church? 8 Reasons why you must attend Church.
- Freedom from Condemnation -- Breaking free from the burden and weight of sin.
- I cannot serve a big God and remain small
- How to start your own business
- How to Make Godly Decisions
- How to Avoid Financial Collapse
- Let Brotherly Love Continue: An insight into love and companionship.
- Breaking Out of the Debt Trap
- Common Causes of Unanswered Prayer.
- How to Argue with God and Win -- Biblical strategies on getting God's attention for all your circumstances all of the time

- Avoiding Power Failure-- How to generate spiritual power for daily success and victorious living.
- How Long Should I Continue to Pray when I Don't See an Answer?
- Success Killers: Seven Habits of Highly Ineffective Christians.
- The Financial Resource Handbook – UK Edition
- Divine Strategies for Uncommon Breakthroughs: Living in the Reality of the Supernatural
- Keys to Divine Success
- Wrong Thoughts, Wrong Emotions and Wrong Living
- Secrets of Biblical Wealth Transfer
- Journey to Fulfillment
- Prosperity Unleashed – A Definitive Guide to Biblical Economics
- No More Debt – Volume 1
- Understanding Dominion
- Advancement
- Getting the Story Straight
- Overcoming when Overwhelmed

- The Spiritual Fitness Plan
- Spiritual and Practical Steps to Command Value
- Breakthrough Strategies for Christians in the Marketplace

For more information about our ministry, world outreaches and a free catalogue of our media and study materials, please write to:

Winning Faith Outreach Ministries
151 Mackenzie Road
London. N7 8NF
UNITED KINGDOM
www.charlesomole.com

Email: **Info@Charlesomole.com**

Breakthrough Strategies for Christians in the Marketplace

Divine Strategies on Living above the World's System and enjoy the days of Heaven on Earth.

UNDERSTANDING DOMINION

CHARLES OMOLE
AUTHOR: "SECRETS OF BIBLICAL WEALTH TRANSFER"

Breakthrough Strategies for Christians in the Marketplace

A Definitive Christian Guide
to Biblical Economics

PROSPERITY Unleashed

Charles Omole

Breakthrough Strategies for Christians in the Marketplace

Book Coming Soon...

www.ingramcontent.com/pod-product-compliance
Lightning Source LLC
Chambersburg PA
CBHW032058090426
42743CB00007B/164